A

SOUTHERN
GENTLEMAN'S
KITCHEN

Southern Living®

Adventures in Cooking, Eating, and Living in the New South

A SOUTHERN GENTLEMAN'S KITCHEN

MATT MOORE

Oxmoor House®

CONTENTS

FOREWORD

Good food, good drink, and good conversation served as the three pillars of Southern hospitality for hundreds of years, and Matt Moore has helped bring these classic elements into the 21st century. Matt knows the manners of the warm and welcoming gentleman never go out of style and that still today—perhaps especially today—nothing makes a guest feel more at ease than a cold drink, a belly full of warm food, and an engaging yarn.

Matt's ability to be inspired by his Southern heritage while updating its traditions has made him the perfect contributing food editor for my blog, The Art of Manliness, which makes its aim to wed the best of the past with the best of the present. In *A Southern Gentleman's Kitchen*, Matt doesn't just write recipes, but shares the stories that go with each one. You hang out in the kitchen with him, you join him on the sidelines of his high school football games, for a Sunday supper with his family, on a wild boar hunt, and more. With his recipes, Matt invites you to pull up a chair at his table, relax, and check out what's simmering on the stove.

Matt's ability for putting you at ease doesn't end with his stories, either; he has a way of making cooking approachable, and yes, even manly. The recipes are simple and tasty, and his directions for making them are friendly and accessible. He'll put his arm around you, guide you through the process, and let you know "You can do this."

Finally, Matt helps you understand why you ought to give this cooking business a try in the first place. He never tires of illuminating the ways that cooking is a gentlemanly skill—how it fosters autonomy, keeps you healthier, impresses the ladies, and provides tasty sustenance to others. Matt helps the average guy be able to see himself in the kitchen. And his way of evocatively painting the benefits of breaking bread with friends and family inspires you to serve home-cooked meals to those you love.

Matt has helped hundreds of thousands of Art of Manliness readers slow down, discover their inner Southern gentleman, and with *A Southern Gentleman's Kitchen* you, too, will discover this plus the satisfaction of fresh food shared with good friends. Hospitality never goes out of style, and neither will this cookbook.

Brett McKay,
Creator and editor of The Art of Manliness
artofmanliness.com

From
A SOUTHERN GENTLEMAN'S KITCHEN

To write a book on Southern cuisine is no easy endeavor. Honestly, it's taken many handles of bourbon, late nights, endless miles, damn good food, repeat tracks from The Marshall Tucker Band, and passionate collaboration with family, friends, and strangers to put this book in your hands. This is my lifestyle. This is my South.

The difficulty of writing such a book lies in the fact that our beloved cuisine is not easily defined, for it varies greatly by region, culture, and experience. Try to get ten Southerners to agree on the proper way to smoke a pork shoulder, and you're likely to receive ten different, fiercely-debated responses. As it is with such tried-and-true dishes, down here everyone has an opinion or two on the best way to go about such things. In the end, and regardless of the recipe that makes the final cut, I'm willing to wager that all ten plates of smoked pulled pork will be eagerly devoured, appropriately sopped up with white bread, and served with a smattering of dill pickles and a bottle or three of cold beer. Naturally, the conversation and fellowship around the table will be just as lively and spirited as the savory meal because that's the very heart of Southern cuisine and culture—cooking and sharing our food and having a damn good time doing it. Cooking has always been an important tradition in my family. Some might go so far as to call it an obsession. I recall my mama's mama, Sitty, as she was known, frying chicken early Sunday morning before hurrying off to dress and head for church. Practically ravenous, we would all return home—family, friends, preachers, and anyone else who wanted to join—to find a bounty of food that seemed like it stretched the length of the Mississippi—fried chicken, cornbread, turnip greens, roasted beets, snap beans, pole beans, purple hulled peas, mashed potatoes, sliced tomatoes, and macaroni and cheese.

Better yet, since my grandfather, Giddy, was the local butcher and market proprietor in Valdosta, Georgia, there

The South Georgia secret, Sitty's Fried Chicken

were always a few select "butcher cuts" of beef reserved for the gentleman's table. Apparently, it was this Southern splendor of Sunday foods that inspired Daddy to ask for Mama's hand in marriage, which is now four decades strong, I might add. To this day, I've never eaten a better piece of fried chicken than my Sitty's. Its juicy, tender meat is perfectly surrounded with a light, crispy crust. And now you have this well-guarded South Georgia secret recipe (see page 101). Who knows...love might even follow.

ENTERPRISE, MISSISSIPPI

Some 450 miles down the road from Valdosta, Daddy's parents raised cattle and kids in the small town of Enterprise, Mississippi. On this farm, Daddy first taught me the Xs and Os of cattle breeding, firing a shotgun, cane-pole catfish fishing, and the sting of a spanking that resulted from stealing Papa's chewing tobacco. Nannie and Papa's farm and their quiet, country town were quite a departure from our suburban Atlanta upbringing, yet the time I spent in those beautiful fields and the dark, serene pines built an enduring foundation for my youth. Memories like watching my sister, Ashley, learning how to drive a straight shift truck through a cow pasture—or aiming rounds at old Dr Pepper® 10 2 4 glass bottles are some of my fondest.

For Daddy's family, food was much less of a cultural experience than Mama's. My father considers himself a "meat and potatoes" kind of guy. That being said, Nannie had a trick or two up her culinary sleeve, including her scrumptious

Caramel Cake (see page 241). Whenever I prepare these recipes, it reminds me of her grace and generosity—something I think all of us can draw upon whenever our grandmas' recipes make an appearance in our own kitchens.

As it is, I learned to cook the "old-fashioned way" in the best of all kitchens—Mama's. I remember nightly routines of coming home from football practice, throwing my clothes in the laundry (she taught me that, too), and standing side by side with Mama prepping, chopping, cooking, and stirring. That nightly ritual of preparing the family meal with Mama allowed me to learn the traditions and techniques passed down by the generations that came before us. Y'all will see in this book that my cuisine is steeped in Southern tradition, yet undeniably influenced by my Mediterranean and Middle Eastern ancestry. Although such cooking influences are now all the rage amongst the culinary scenesters, I'm pretty sure my family was the first to discover the unbelievably awesome pairing of fried chicken with tabbouleh!

On that note, there's quite a buzz these days about the South. I hear terms like "Farm to Table," "Locavore," and "Catch to Plate" almost ad nauseam. Truth be told, my Great-grandmother Addie, who maintained a garden well into her nineties, would have found these expressions rather amusing. Cooking in season, living off the farm, and knowing the source of one's ingredients is simply the way we've always done things down here. Still, I'm happy to see that so many folks are uniting around authenticity.

Passion for great food and ingredients is a theme you'll find in each and every one of

Welcome to my kitchen!

my storied recipes. Mama might have been my culinary mentor, but Daddy was the one who taught me about having passion and pride in every element of life. I learned the values of hard work and persistence from Daddy when I was on the baseball and football fields trying to master a circle changeup and tackle a running back. Not one to preach or lecture, Daddy always demonstrated his leadership through action. After long weeks of working on the road to provide for our family, Daddy still found time to cut the grass for the single mom next door and drop off the elderly

My grandfather, Giddy, butchering meats at the family store.

ladies at early church before sitting down with us for a family Sunday breakfast of country ham and drop biscuits (just you wait till you try these). Though he did not seek recognition, Daddy's leadership and self-sacrifice to aid and serve others created a lasting impression on me.

THE REAL WORLD

When I left to attend college (Go Dawgs!), I discovered that my experiences at home and my obsession surrounding food were not the norm. Despite the fact that most of us watched a lot of food television shows, nearly everyone I knew, men and women alike, lacked the basic skills to pull off wholesome, home-cooked meals. The majority of my friends came from families where cooking was not a central activity at home. In fact, most of the meals they ate while they were at college were takeout, processed frozen entrées, or off the menu

at restaurants in town. To be fair, my friends turned out just fine (well, most of them).

Regardless, I began my culinary crusade by inviting friends over for dinner, financing my parties by playing guitar and singing in bars in downtown Athens, Georgia. My friends took an interest in not only the free meals, but also my simple, straightforward instructions. We drank a ton of wine, stayed up too late, and told stories about the glory days when we played football at Parkview High School... at least to those who would listen. Those four years of home-cooked meals and parties around my "family table" established friendships and connections that still remain strong.

Then came the real world. With new jobs and the prospect of climbing the corporate ladder, my friends fell right back into their same rotgut, takeout routines. I get it—preparing a meal might feel inconvenient at times, especially when life and work demands seem to spiral out of control. But—and I said this to them—just allow yourself this image: the repetitive sounds of chopping, steam rising out of pots and pans, and sizzling meats over an open flame, coupled with a good glass (or two) of wine in hand. In the end, you will have conceptualized, executed, and created something entirely your own, which is one of the greatest forms of fulfillment that results from simply spending more time cooking. You see, I believe you can become a better version of yourself by spending more time in the most unlikely of all places—the kitchen! This book will teach you that cooking can stimulate creativity and provide more satisfaction in your daily life than you ever thought possible.

Just think of the satisfaction you will feel from gathering your family and friends around your table and experiencing their delight in the food you serve them—because you have given love and passion to prepare your best.

SIMPLY SOUTHERN

Allow this book to serve as my (in)formal invitation for you to have a seat at my kitchen table. You see, my cooking philosophy revolves around the fact that one does not need to have formal training or a lengthy list of pricey ingredients to prepare and create remarkable meals. After all, I'm not a chef! With the exception of a slight Southern drawl, I will not confuse you with hard-to-pronounce ingredients, nor will I set you up for failure with recipes that are tailored for experts. In fact, I've been very careful to include the dishes that have met the strictest of standards—only those that I serve to friends and family around my table. Pardon my vernacular, but if it ain't good enough for them, then it ain't good enough for you, either!

I believe that Southern cuisine can be prepared quite simply and healthfully. Sure, you'll find butter, bacon, and cream in my recipes, and I'll even show you how to deep-fry a crawfish tail or two. I want to help you discover that cooking is actually more of an adventure than a task. The way I see it, whether the ingredients are hunted, caught, raised, or simply acquired at a local market, much of the fulfillment that comes from preparing meals lies miles away from any stovetop. Cooking offers us the chance to satisfy man's

primal instinct to provide. That's a nightly lesson I live out each time I cook for my beautiful wife, Callie, at our home in east Nashville, Tennessee. She is my inspiration, my best friend, and of course, the most beautiful "recipe tester" in all of God's country…the South! For me, a home-cooked meal is a modern-day expression of chivalry that goes a country mile.

I'll be the first to tell you gents that women don't care if your recipe is always a home run. In fact, sometimes it may fall totally flat. Hey, that's okay. As Daddy would say, "Get up, and try, try again, Son." I'm here to tell you guys that it's all about putting a bit of effort into doing something out of the ordinary for that special person in your life. A woman wants a man who pursues and understands her heart, and a man must be willing to take on a bit of risk and adventure to capture said heart. Think of the kitchen as a modern stage for you to demonstrate your sense of confidence, care, and precision to that lovely woman. Trust me—you'll capture the heart of your loved one when you whip up my comforting, indulgent Pasta Bolognese (see page 171).

Cooking great food also provides us with an opportunity to share and invest in one of the South's best-regarded characteristics—to be hospitable. I strive daily to practice such Southern hospitality, to be polite, engaging, and gracious. I encourage you to use this book not only as your template to great meals, but also as a resource to start inviting friends and strangers to have a seat at your family table.

In the meantime, come along and meet some great characters, friends, and family who serve as my culinary inspiration—from Ernest Pillow, my favorite cabbie, and his famous ribs, to super star Luke Bryan's celebrated fish fry and Mama's amazing carrot cake. The lesson is that life and food are best when shared. I'll serve as your culinary guide down the dirt roads of Alabama to the eight-lane superhighways of Atlanta. We'll fry Mississippi catfish, perfect Charleston's famous shrimp and grits, uncover the artistry of pickling and preserving, low and slow barbecue, cast-iron cooking, and so many more of the South's curiosities. Of course, we'll sip plenty of Tennessee moonshine and experience the sweet, smoky flavors of Kentucky small batch bourbon.

THE "NEW SOUTH"

Y'all will learn that our "New South" cuisine is as embodied in our flourishing Southern cities as it is along the back roads of Appalachia. Within the pages of this book are the people, places, and

stories that inspire my recipes. So come and share my passion for good food and revelry. Let's get our hands in the dirt and on the flesh of those great ingredients—from Louisiana redfish to Georgia olive oil—that span the Southern landscape. I will introduce you to artisans, farmers, shrimp boat captains, writers, musicians, and artists, those good folk throughout the South who make our world a bit simpler and a whole lot richer. Together we'll pay homage to a culture filled with tradition and folklore, while cooking up some mighty tasty and delectable dishes that you will be proud to serve to your family and friends. Together we shall live, eat, cook, drink, and learn!

Go ahead and pour yourself a tall glass (three-fingers high and neat, of course) of Tennessee whiskey. Take your shoes off, and stay awhile. It's my pleasure to welcome you to *A Southern Gentleman's Kitchen*.

A SOUTHERN GENTLEMAN IS

Hospitable	Generous
Adventurous	Humble
Self-Sacrificing	Respectful
Chivalrous	Worldly
Intellectually Curious	Appreciative

SOUTHERN SPLENDOR

If Twain said the way things were cooked in the South of his boyhood was the main splendor, by now our pickin's have pickled into a Southern splendor all their own, known now more than ever before, particularly certain dishes, particularly so because the way things cook down here:

Buttermilk battered catfish reeled in not an hour before frying alongside frog legs gigged by us kids the night before,

Okra and cornmeal fritter to be forked over first to hush up us puppies, pestering about, downwind the wafting collard green pot, tortured in pangs from the pan-sizzling cornbread,

Venison tenderloin thawed and seasoned from last season grilling beneath Worcestershire-butter'd sweet onions—of Vidalia, of course—and vats of boiling peanuts and bubbling Brunswick or rabbit stew (depending how the beagles ran that day).

On ice, cold as they come, blue-ribbon canned brew cooler'd side-by-side. Coleslaw of culinary delight, potato salad of the mustardly make, jugged sweet tea to drink, and watermelon to spit seeds and suck;

Tabled atop, much too high to reach, Muscadine wine bottled and sipped slow by the belles before they bade us adieu,

And the card playing became real with unearthed bourbon unsealed when cigar charm would perk my young ears to the same stories heard told and retold in melodies, intonations and elisions our own—Southern Splendor! O South-uhn Splendah!—by and in the company of great men, most of whom are gone, but live on in toast...

To the Southern gentlemen
and the grand traditions of his makeshift kitchen!

By C.B. Ozburn — Southern Folklorist

TO START +
TO SHARE

Black-eyed Pea Hummus

You can find this hummus in my fridge 24/7—it takes just five minutes to make. Once you've done it, you'll forget about buying those pricey small containers at the store. Instead of chickpeas, I like subbing a classic Southern ingredient, black-eyed peas, which yields a hummus that is a bit darker in color and also nuttier in taste—both of which I find to be incredibly delicious.

For the health-conscious among your guests, you can serve this alongside some cut up carrots, celery, peppers, cucumbers, and tomatoes. It's also nice to indulge with whole-grain crackers or some warmed toasted pita bread, sliced into triangles for dipping.

HANDS-ON 5 MIN. TOTAL 5 MIN.

MAKES 1¾ CUPS

1 Process first 5 ingredients and 1 Tbsp. oil in a food processor until smooth and blended.

2 Add tahini and 1 Tbsp. water, and process until blended, adding more water, 1 tsp. at a time, until desired consistency.

3 Spoon into a small serving bowl, and drizzle with remaining 1 Tbsp. olive oil.

INGREDIENTS

1 (15.8-oz.) can black-eyed peas, rinsed and drained
2 garlic cloves, minced
3 Tbsp. fresh lemon juice
¼ tsp. kosher salt
⅛ tsp. ground cumin
2 Tbsp. extra virgin olive oil, divided
2 Tbsp. tahini
Garnish: smoked paprika

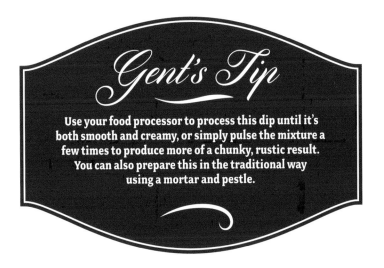

Gent's Tip

Use your food processor to process this dip until it's both smooth and creamy, or simply pulse the mixture a few times to produce more of a chunky, rustic result. You can also prepare this in the traditional way using a mortar and pestle.

Pan-Seared Sea Scallops

I love that this dish is all about high-quality ingredients and keeping things simple—and requires no extra salt or seasoning. Instead, I let the salt-cured flavors from the pancetta drippings and the bright acidity from the lemon do all of the work. Sea scallops are one of my favorite foods, period. I love getting a bit of char on the outside to enhance the flavor, while leaving the tender meat cooked just to medium. And pancetta, which is basically the Italian form of bacon that hasn't been smoked, is perfect because its mild flavor doesn't overpower the scallops' delicate sweetness. This simple yet impressive appetizer pairs well with a cold lager or a crisp, dry white wine.

HANDS-ON **12 MIN.** TOTAL **12 MIN.**

SERVES **4**

⇒ INGREDIENTS ⇐

1 (2-oz.) pancetta slab (not thinly sliced), finely chopped
12 sea scallops (about 1 lb.)
1 tsp. unsalted butter
1 tsp. extra virgin olive oil
1 Tbsp. fresh lemon juice
Garnish: fresh parsley leaves

1 Heat a 12-inch cast-iron skillet over medium heat 1 minute. Add pancetta, and cook, stirring occasionally, 5 minutes or until crisp. Remove pancetta using a slotted spoon, and drain on paper towels, reserving drippings in skillet.

2 Pat scallops dry with paper towels. Melt butter with oil and reserved drippings in skillet over medium-high heat; add scallops, and cook on 1 side 1 minute (do not touch). Turn scallops, sprinkle with lemon juice, and cook 1½ minutes or just until scallops are just firm to the touch. Remove from heat.

3 Spoon scallops onto serving plates, and drizzle with pan drippings. Sprinkle with pancetta, and serve immediately.

Creole Popcorn

Most of my college experience was spent playing music in the many bars and clubs that litter the downtown scene of Athens, Georgia. From the Georgia Theatre and Boar's Head Lounge to Tasty World and the 40 Watt Club—we played 'em all. Athens is known throughout the country for boasting a vibrant, if not eclectic, music scene that has spawned the likes of R.E.M., Widespread Panic, and Neutral Milk Hotel, as well as more recent acts like the Drive-By Truckers and my friends The Whigs. Bissett's was my favorite downtown destination and that's why I like to remake my version of their classic Creole popcorn—deep-fried crawfish tails served with a creamy caper rémoulade. Most grocers sell frozen crawfish tails in the freezer section—thaw them under some cold running water and pat dry, and you are ready to go. Crack open a cold Abita Amber to get the full experience!

HANDS-ON 25 MIN. TOTAL 30 MIN.

SERVES 4

⇒ INGREDIENTS ⇐

Peanut oil
2 large eggs, beaten
¼ cup milk
1 lb. frozen cooked, peeled crawfish tails, thawed and drained
1 cup all-purpose flour
½ cup plain yellow cornmeal
1½ tsp. Creole seasoning
Rémoulade

1 Pour oil to a depth of 1½ inches into a 12-inch cast-iron skillet. Heat oil over medium heat to 350°.

2 Stir together eggs and milk in a medium bowl. Stir in crawfish, and let stand 5 minutes. Combine flour, cornmeal, and seasoning in a separate bowl. Remove crawfish from egg mixture, discarding egg mixture. Toss crawfish in flour mixture until coated. Shake off excess flour, leaving a very light coating.

3 Fry crawfish, in 3 batches, 2 minutes or until golden brown. (Crawfish will rise to top of oil when thoroughly cooked.) Drain on paper towels. Serve hot crawfish immediately with Rémoulade.

Rémoulade

HANDS-ON 5 MIN. TOTAL 5 MIN.

MAKES ⅓ CUP

⇒ INGREDIENTS ⇐

¼ cup mayonnaise
1 tsp. Creole seasoning
1 tsp. Creole or whole grain mustard
1 tsp. prepared horseradish
1 tsp. drained capers, chopped
1 tsp. fresh lemon juice
¼ tsp. hot sauce

1 Stir together all ingredients in a small bowl until thoroughly blended. Cover and chill until ready to serve.

THE CLASSIC CITY — ATHENS, GA

Music ain't the only thing going on in Athens, Georgia. The food is equally on par. A beloved institution that existed for quite a while on Broad Street, Harry Bissett's New Orleans Café, was a personal favorite. Flush with five crisp $20 bills from playing a club the night before, I felt as rich as a Wall Street trader when I'd walk into their doors to snag lunch before an accounting class on north campus. Let's put it this way—there weren't a lot of college kids splurging for a lunch at Bissett's during a casual Tuesday, so instead I made friends with the older regulars at the bar listening to jazz, talking literature, and, of course, wondering when and if that elusive national championship would ever return to Old Glory.

After a po'boy and a few Abita Ambers, I'd depart one world of pleasure into the doldrums of Generally Accepted Accounting Principles and financial reconciliation. Ah, to only be back at Bissett's.

Deviled Eggs

Here are 3 variations on a Southern classic. To start, hard-boil your eggs. For a dozen eggs, place eggs in a single layer in a large saucepan, and add enough water to cover by 1 inch. Bring the water to a rolling boil; cover, remove from heat, and let stand 12 minutes. Then drain immediately, and return eggs to pan. Fill pan with cold water and ice. Cover the pan, and shake vigorously to crack eggs all over. Peel under cold running water.

+ Crispy Bacon

HANDS-ON 10 MIN.   TOTAL 22 MIN.
MAKES 1 DOZ.

≽ INGREDIENTS ≼

4 bacon slices
6 large hard-cooked eggs, peeled
2 Tbsp. plus 1½ tsp. mayonnaise
2 Tbsp. finely chopped dill pickle
⅛ tsp. cracked black pepper
⅛ tsp. kosher salt
Finely chopped chives

1 Preheat oven to 375°. Arrange bacon in a single layer on a wire rack in a shallow pan. Bake 12 minutes or until bacon is browned and crispy, turning once halfway through. Remove bacon, and drain on paper towels.

2 Slice eggs in half lengthwise, and carefully remove yolks. Using a wire whisk or a fork, mash yolks with mayonnaise and next 3 ingredients in a small bowl until blended.

3 Place egg white halves on a serving platter, and spoon or pipe yolk mixture into egg white halves. Break each bacon slice into thirds, and stand a bacon piece in filling of each. Sprinkle with chopped chives, and serve immediately.

Note: Tested with Benton's bacon.

Cajun Style

HANDS-ON 15 MIN.   TOTAL 15 MIN.
MAKES 1 DOZ.

≽ INGREDIENTS ≼

⅓ lb. andouille sausage, cut into
    12 (⅓-inch-thick) slices
6 large hard-cooked eggs, peeled
2½ Tbsp. mayonnaise
2 Tbsp. minced capers
⅛ tsp. Cajun seasoning

1 Place a medium skillet over medium heat 1 minute or until hot. Add sausage, and cook, stirring occasionally, 4-6 minutes or until browned. Drain on paper towels.

2 Slice eggs in half lengthwise, and carefully remove yolks. Using a wire whisk or a fork, mash yolks with mayonnaise, capers, and seasoning in a small bowl until blended.

3 Place egg white halves on a serving platter, and spoon or pipe yolk mixture into egg white halves. Top each with a sausage slice, and serve immediately.

+ Pimiento Cheese

HANDS-ON 15 MIN. **TOTAL 15 MIN.**

MAKES 1 DOZ.

1 Combine sliced jalapeño and red wine vinegar in a 1-cup glass measuring cup, and let stand 5 minutes.

2 Meanwhile, slice eggs in half lengthwise, and carefully remove yolks. Using a wire whisk or a fork, mash yolks with mayonnaise and next 4 ingredients in a small bowl until blended.

3 Place egg white halves on a serving platter, and spoon or pipe yolk mixture into egg white halves. Drain jalapeño slices, and pat dry with paper towels. Carefully place 1 jalapeño slice on each egg, and serve immediately.

⇒ INGREDIENTS ⇐

1 jalapeño pepper, seeded and
  very thinly sliced
2 Tbsp. red wine vinegar
6 large hard-cooked eggs, peeled
3 Tbsp. mayonnaise
1 Tbsp. diced pimiento
2 Tbsp. (½ oz.) finely shredded sharp
  white Cheddar cheese
⅛ tsp. kosher salt
⅛ tsp. cracked black pepper

Boiled Peanuts

Throughout the South, you'll find truck stops, gas stations, and produce stands right off the highway serving up boiled peanuts out of a cast-iron cauldron or a 50-gallon drum. These guys are absolutely addicting, which is why I always stop whenever I see a hand-painted sign on the side of the road advertising "Hot Boiled Peanuts."

Raw "green" peanuts are best for this recipe, and they are harvested from May through September. Be sure to soak and thoroughly wash them before bringing them to slow-boiled goodness.

HANDS-ON 10 MIN. TOTAL 4 HR., 30 MIN.
MAKES 14 CUPS

INGREDIENTS

2 lbs. raw peanuts in the shell
½-¾ cup kosher salt

1 Soak peanuts in warm water to cover in a large stockpot 20 minutes to loosen any dirt. Drain peanuts, working in batches, if necessary. Rinse peanuts under cold running water, shaking vigorously to remove any dirt or grit.

2 Place peanuts and desired amount of kosher salt in a 6-qt. Dutch oven, and add water to cover (I add enough salt for the mixture to taste like saltwater.) Bring to a boil over high heat. Cover, reduce heat to low, and simmer, stirring occasionally, 4 hours or until peanuts are tender, yet still firm enough to hold their shape when shelled, adding water as needed to keep peanuts covered. Serve hot, at room temperature, or chilled.

Pimiento Cheese Crostini

Down South, "p'mennacheese" rolls off many a tongue. I prefer to go easy on the "love," mayonnaise, and focus my efforts by using top-quality sharp Cheddar. Check out Kenny's Farmhouse Cheese in Austin, Kentucky, for some of the best cheese in the South (see page 278). Pimiento cheese can be made up to three days in advance and kept covered in the refrigerator and should yield enough leftovers for lunch or a late-night sandwich.

HANDS-ON 18 MIN. TOTAL 28 MIN.
SERVES 6-8

INGREDIENTS

1 (16-oz.) block sharp Cheddar cheese,
  at room temperature
¼ Vidalia or sweet onion
1 (4-oz.) can diced pimiento, drained
½ cup mayonnaise
⅛ tsp. ground red pepper
1 (12-oz.) French bread baguette,
  cut into 50 (¼-inch-thick) slices
6 Tbsp. olive oil
½ tsp. freshly ground black pepper
Garnish: finely chopped fresh chives

1 Preheat oven to 400°. Shred cheese through large holes of a box grater. Grate onion through small holes of grater to equal 1 tsp.; squeeze grated onion in a paper towel to remove excess moisture. Combine cheese, onion, and next 3 ingredients in a large bowl. Using a fork, mash ingredients until cheese softens and mixture is thoroughly blended.

2 Place bread slices in a single layer on a baking sheet. Generously brush tops of bread slices with oil, and sprinkle with freshly ground black pepper. Bake at 400° for 10 minutes or until edges are golden brown.

3 Spread cheese mixture generously over tops of toasted bread slices, and serve immediately.

Gent's Tip

Cooking times vary significantly so I like to check the peanuts after the first 2 hours and every 30 minutes thereafter. That also gives me a good excuse to crack open a cold beer and sample my work! Add extra flavor by stirring Creole seasoning, ground red pepper, smoked ham hocks, onion, garlic, or another tasty ingredient into the mixture before bringing it to a boil.

Salt + Pepper Chicken Wings

I'm pretty sure chicken wings are the greatest of all foods to accompany a day of watching sports. Fortunately, I've hosted many games to perfect this staple. I like to keep it simple—this recipe features only three ingredients, and by seasoning the chicken with salt and pepper, you really allow the chicken (and the recipe technique) to speak for itself—but you could certainly toss these in any hot wing or barbecue sauce you might like when they come off the grill. These are best paired with a few of your buddies and a round or two of cold beers. Whip up a batch of these for the big game, and I promise that your friends will name you MVP, regardless if your team of choice wins or loses.

HANDS-ON 22 MIN. **TOTAL 22 MIN.**

SERVES 4

⇒ INGREDIENTS ⇐

24 chicken wings and drummettes (3 lb.)
2 tsp. kosher salt
1½ tsp. freshly ground black pepper

1 Preheat grill to 350°-400° (medium-high). Sprinkle both sides of chicken with salt and pepper.

2 Grill chicken, covered with grill lid, 20 minutes or until skin is crispy and charred, turning every 3-4 minutes. Toss chicken in your favorite sauce, if desired, and serve immediately.

Dixie Antipasto

This platter combines several of my favorite items into one harmonious note—fatty smoked sausage with rich, sharp Cheddar cheese, all perfectly balanced against spicy pepperoncini peppers and whole grain mustard, and served with a side of saltine crackers. Whether you choose to eat each component separately or make perfect bites with everything on the platter, you are starting your meal off right.

HANDS-ON 20 MIN. **TOTAL 20 MIN.**
SERVES 6

1 Preheat grill to 350°-400° (medium-high), or heat a grill pan over medium-high heat. Grill sausage 5 minutes on each side or until slightly charred and grill marks appear. Cut sausage diagonally into 1-inch pieces. Place on a large platter or serving plate.

2 Arrange cheese, peppers, and crackers on platter with sausage. Serve immediately with mustard.

Note: Tested with Conecuh Hickory Smoked Sausage.

⇉ INGREDIENTS ⇇

1 lb. hickory-smoked sausage
1 (8-oz.) block sharp Cheddar cheese, diced into 1-inch cubes
1 (16-oz.) jar pepperoncini salad peppers, drained
1 sleeve saltine crackers
¼ cup whole grain mustard

DAVE HAYWOOD

Dave Haywood, guitarist for the hit group Lady Antebellum, was on his way to becoming an accountant when he decided to pursue his stage dreams with childhood buddy Charles Kelley. This was years ago, and, at the time, I'd had some experience in the music biz, so a mutual friend suggested that Dave look me up. Quitting a steady career in accounting to chase the noise was a far departure for Dave, the son of a dentist from Augusta, Georgia.

Years later, he laughingly tells me that his Mama and Daddy supported his decision as best they could, which meant sending him as many prayers as possible. I'm proud to say I was also there to lend my support at the start—through emails, I offered advice on touring and booking shows. I called up my good friend Warren Southall to book one of Dave and Charles' early gigs at Walkers in Athens, Georgia, selling Warren on the fact that the boys would play for a cut of the door and a few cold beers. What a poor agent I would have made!

On a recent morning, Dave, whose Grammy-winning group now sells out arenas from New York to Australia, and I are sitting in my kitchen hoping to accomplish more important things... recreating the famous egg salad sandwiches served at Augusta National, home to the Masters golf tournament and also where Dave grew up.

It turns out that Dave is quite the egg-salad expert, having spent his high-school years peddling humble egg salad and pimento cheese sandwiches to hungry spectators. Though the sport of golf is always at the forefront of the Masters, it's the humble food behind the scenes that also garners praise, made even better by the fact that sandwiches and beers can be purchased for just a few bucks—a rarity at premiere sporting events nowadays. You might say that such humbleness is what defines Dave Haywood—as a Southern gentleman, he's also patient, respectful, and professional. And though egg salad is the dish on the menu today, Dave is no stranger to the kitchen. After some testing and debate (and a few mimosas), here's our tribute to sport, food, and humility, all wrapped up in one delicious bite. Fore!

Egg Salad Sandwiches

I don't know exactly what's in the egg salad at Augusta National Golf Club and to be honest, I don't want to know—the mystery is what keeps it fun. In my version, I like mustard and dill pickle relish, which add a bit of bite and texture. To get that perfectly smooth texture, I finely grate the eggs and mash everything with a fork until well combined. To keep it even more real, serve it just like they do on the course in a super-thin plastic green baggie—not easy to find.

HANDS-ON 15 MIN. TOTAL 15 MIN.

MAKES 20 FINGER SANDWICHES

1 Using a fork, mash first 6 ingredients in a large bowl until mixture is thoroughly blended and smooth.

2 Spread a generous layer of egg mixture on 1 side of 5 bread slices; top with remaining bread slices. Cut each sandwich into 4 finger sandwiches, and serve immediately.

⟩ INGREDIENTS ⟨

12 hard-cooked eggs, peeled and finely grated

½ cup mayonnaise

1 Tbsp. finely chopped dill pickle

1 tsp. kosher salt

1 tsp. yellow mustard

¾ tsp. freshly ground black pepper

10 slices white bread, crusts removed

Fried Dill Pickle Chips + Cayenne Dipping Sauce

Sure, soaking pickles in buttermilk, dredging them in flour, and deep-frying 'em in peanut oil might be gluttonous, but it tastes so damn good. That being said, this dish can be prepared quickly, and it's the perfect appetizer to share with all your hungry friends, as I often do when I'm deep-frying something for the main course such as fried chicken or fish. Yes, I get it, that's quite a bit of deep-fried goodness, but we aren't counting calories. Besides, if I'm gonna break out that heavy cast-iron pan and fill it with oil, I like it to perform double duty by serving up a couple of courses!

I use dill pickle chips instead of whole pickles as I find it's much easier to get that crispy texture. And to me, there's no better pickle coming out of the South than Phickles Pickles, handmade in Athens, Georgia, by Angie Tillman (see page 278). Paired up with the heat from the cayenne pepper in the dipping sauce, I challenge you to eat just one. Trust me, ain't gonna happen.

HANDS-ON 22 MIN. TOTAL **22 MIN.**

SERVES 6

⇒ INGREDIENTS ⇐

1 (16-oz.) jar dill pickle chips
¾ cup Ranch dressing
¼ tsp. ground cayenne pepper
2 dashes of hot sauce
Peanut oil
1 cup buttermilk
1 large egg
1¼ cups all-purpose flour
1 tsp. Creole seasoning

1 Drain pickles, reserving 1 tsp. pickle juice. Stir together reserved pickle juice, dressing, cayenne pepper, and hot sauce in a small bowl until blended. Cover dipping sauce, and chill until ready to serve.

2 Pour oil to a depth of 1½ inches in a 12-inch cast-iron skillet. Heat oil over medium heat to 350°.

3 Preheat oven to 200°. Whisk together buttermilk and egg in a large bowl; stir in drained pickles. Stir together flour and Creole seasoning in a large shallow dish. Remove 10 pickles from buttermilk mixture; dredge in flour mixture, shaking off any excess. Fry pickles in hot oil 3-4 minutes or until golden brown. Drain pickles on a paper towel–lined plate. Keep warm in a 200° oven. Repeat procedure with remaining pickles and flour mixture in batches of 10.

4 Serve pickles with dipping sauce.

Note: Tested with Tabasco hot sauce.

Raw Apalachicola Oysters + Mignonette

The sweet, meaty oysters from Apalachicola Bay in Florida are considered some of the best in the South—if not the world. Fortunately these specific bivalves were my first foray into slurping down these delicious treats, and though I've since tasted them fresh from Prince Edward Island to the south of France, I must admit I'm partial to Apalachicola oysters. But these delicacies are becoming more rare these days as the freshwater Chattahoochee and Flint Rivers, which provide the natural habitat for the oysters, are subject to litigation by both the Florida and Georgia state legislatures. Since these taste so good without any help from cocktail sauce or crackers, I like serving them with a simple mignonette, which brings out their briny, sweet flavors.

HANDS-ON 20 MIN. TOTAL 1 HR.

SERVES 4

1 Shuck oysters, reserving bottom shell and discarding top shell. Spread rock salt on a serving tray, and place shucked oysters in shells on rock salt.

2 Whisk together vinegar and next 3 ingredients in a bowl until blended. Serve mignonette sauce with oysters.

INGREDIENTS

1 dozen Apalachicola oysters in the shell
Rock salt
4 Tbsp. red wine vinegar
1 Tbsp. plus 1½ tsp. finely minced shallot
⅛ tsp. kosher salt
½ tsp. freshly ground black pepper

Gent's Tips

HOW TO SHUCK AN OYSTER
1. Secure the top and bottom of the oyster on a towel against a hard surface.
2. Insert an oyster knife into the 'key' or hinge—do not force pressure towards your hand. Instead twist the knife to pop open the shell.
3. Use the knife to remove the top and bottom abductor muscles, remove grit, and serve.

Little Bites of Heaven

No reunion of my family is complete until these delicious treats hit the table. Stuffed grape leaves are from my Mama's side of the family and carry as much pride as does our fried chicken. These are always made best with fresh grape leaves. For that reason, my Sitty always kept vines in her backyard. Fortunately, you can find jarred grape leaves in most supermarkets. Over the years, I've met several friends who also enjoy grape leaves. Of course, we fight over who makes the best version. Some folks like to brown and place thinly sliced pork chops on the bottom of the pot to impart their flavor, while others swear by cooking theirs with a bit of tomato.

Stuffed Grape Leaves

Traditionally, stuffed grape leaves are prepared with ground lamb, but I like to also use ground beef, venison, or even bison as part of my stuffing—whatever I have in my freezer, and I like to make a big batch to serve warm or at room temperature. They go nicely as part of an antipasto platter or alongside the main dish.

HANDS-ON 52 MIN. **TOTAL 2 HR., 9 MIN.**

SERVES 8

1 Prepare Stuffing: Stir together ground chuck and next 8 ingredients in a large bowl until well blended. (Be careful not to overwork mixture.)

2 Prepare Grape Leaves: Rinse grape leaves, and thoroughly pat dry with paper towels. Remove and discard stems. Layer 10 leaves and half of thinly sliced garlic in a 3-qt. Dutch oven or medium-size heavy saucepan.

3 Place 1 grape leaf, vein side up, on work surface. Spoon 1 Tbsp. stuffing mixture onto center of grape leaf. Bring 2 opposite points of leaf to center; fold over filling. Beginning at 1 short side, roll up leaf tightly, jelly-roll fashion. Place stuffed grape leaf, seam side down, in Dutch oven. Repeat procedure with grape leaves and stuffing mixture until all stuffing mixture is used, placing rolled leaves side by side and changing position of rolled grape leaves with each layer so that the upper layer is perpendicular to the layer below it. Place any remaining leaves on top of stuffed grape leaves. Sprinkle with remaining garlic, and top with lemon slices. Sprinkle with salt.

4 Add water to Dutch oven until rolled grape leaves are just covered. Place a small heatproof plate on rolled leaves to keep them submerged and prevent them from unrolling during cooking process. Bring to a light boil over medium-high heat; cover, reduce heat to medium-low, and simmer 17 minutes. Turn off heat, leaving Dutch oven on burner; let grape leaves stand, covered, 1 hour before serving. Serve with fresh lemon slices.

STUFFING

1 lb. ground chuck
¾ cup uncooked converted white rice, rinsed
6 garlic cloves, finely minced
2 tsp. kosher salt
1 tsp. freshly ground black pepper
¼ tsp. ground allspice
Dash of ground cinnamon
1 Tbsp. fresh lemon juice
¼ cup unsalted butter, softened

GRAPE LEAVES

2 (8-oz.) jars grape leaves or about 60 fresh grape leaves
4 garlic cloves, thinly sliced
½ lemon, thinly sliced
1 tsp. kosher salt
Fresh lemon slices, to serve

Bacon-Wrapped Duck with Jalapeño + Cream Cheese

Although some find duck meat to be a bit too gamey, I use this recipe as a great introduction to one of my favorite forms of protein—made better with smoky bacon, spicy jalapeño, and rich cream cheese. Nowadays, most grocery stores sell duck breasts either frozen or fresh throughout the year, though I always argue that things taste better when rifled down through your own scope!

These little duck "poppers" are one of my favorite foods for tailgating. I assemble everything before I hit the road for the big game. Once situated, I crack open a cold beer (first things first, right?), fire up the grill, and cook these guys just until the bacon is crispy and cooked through. The next time you are in a quandary over what to serve for the big game, give these a try.

HANDS-ON 45 MIN. TOTAL **2 HR., 15 MIN.**

SERVES 12

INGREDIENTS

¾ cup extra virgin olive oil

¼ cup balsamic vinegar

1 tsp. kosher salt

½ tsp. freshly ground black pepper

¼ tsp. garlic powder

3 lb. skinned and boned duck breasts, cut into 1½-inch pieces

24 center-cut smoked bacon slices, cut in half crosswise

3 large jalapeño peppers, cut into 48 thin slices

1 (8-oz.) package cream cheese

24 (8-inch) wooden skewers

1 Whisk together first 5 ingredients in a shallow dish until blended; add duck, turning to coat. Cover and chill 1-24 hours.

2 Arrange bacon pieces on an aluminum foil-lined baking sheet. Place 1 jalapeño pepper slice on 1 end of each bacon piece. Top each pepper slice with 1 tsp. cream cheese. Chill 30 minutes.

3 Soak wooden skewers in water 30 minutes.

4 Remove duck from marinade, discarding marinade. Place 1 duck piece on cream cheese atop each bacon piece; tightly wrap bacon around duck. Chill 30 minutes. Thread 4 duck bundles onto double skewers (2 skewers side by side), securing bacon and leaving ½-inch space between bundles. Repeat with remaining duck bundles and skewers.

5 Heat 1 side of grill to 350°-400° (medium-high). Arrange skewers over unlit side of grill, and grill, covered with grill lid, 5 minutes on each side or until bacon begins to brown. Transfer to lit side of grill, and grill, covered with grill lid, 2 minutes on each side or until bacon is crisp.

Pan-Fried Bologna Sliders

There's nobody on this planet who loves fried bologna better than my childhood best friend, R.C. Hux. R.C.'s mother, Jamie, often claimed that R.C.'s wedding would feature fried bologna and cheese sandwiches as the main dish.

R.C.'s dad, Richard, is a collector of antiques and guns, a pilot, a fisherman, a car salesman, and a jack-of-all-trades. Saturdays spent with Richard were always an adventure for R.C. and me. We'd visit a flea market to trade coins or art, shoot a tommy gun at an outdoor range, take a tour of the skies in a T-34 airplane, and enjoy a Kentucky Nip soda, all before lunch. When we'd return home after our exploits, Jamie would fix us up a classic fried bologna sandwich. R.C. went with ketchup—but I am a mustard guy. This recipe is the summation of all those great childhood memories in a few fun, tasty bites.

HANDS-ON **13 MIN.** TOTAL **13 MIN.**

SERVES **4**

⇝ INGREDIENTS ⇜

8 small rolls, split
8 thick bologna slices, cut into quarters
4 Tbsp. whole grain mustard
8 dill pickle chips

1 Preheat oven to 400°. Place rolls, cut sides up, on a baking sheet. Bake 6-8 minutes or until lightly toasted.

2 Meanwhile, heat a large skillet over medium heat 1 minute or until hot. Add bologna, and fry 2-3 minutes on each side or until browned. Drain on paper towels.

3 Spread mustard generously on toasted sides of rolls. Layer bologna and pickles on roll bottoms. Cover with roll tops, and serve immediately.

R.C. and I, always up to no good, and R.C. giving the thumbs up as if we were little angels!

Crab Cakes + Caper Rémoulade

Great crab cakes start with great crab. Fortunately, from Maryland and Virginia to the Carolinas and down through the Georgia lowcountry, fresh blue crabs abound in our Southern waters, yielding their sweet, delicious meat serving as the star of this dish. Many folks who live on the coast have a crab trap or two sitting in their garage—it's a requirement of being a true local.

For me, there's nothing more exciting than setting out crab traps at dusk, only to wake up in the morning to haul in the fresh catch. I cook mine up in a big crab boil with friends, reserving any meat for use in this recipe. Of course, you can always purchase fresh cooked crabmeat from your local fishmonger or in your seafood department. In this recipe, I focus most of my efforts on creating just enough of a binder to hold this meat together, without allowing those elements to outshine the meat. Paired up with a creamy, caper rémoulade, this dish is heaven in each bite.

HANDS-ON **24 MIN.**   TOTAL **24 MIN.**

SERVES **4**

1 Prepare Caper Rémoulade: Stir together mayonnaise and next 7 ingredients in a small bowl. Let stand at least 10 minutes before serving. (Rémoulade can be prepared 1 day in advance and refrigerated in an airtight container.)

2 Prepare Crab Cakes: Pick crabmeat, removing any bits of shell. Stir together crab and next 12 ingredients in a large bowl until well blended. Loosely shape mixture into 8 (3-inch) cakes.

3 Heat a 12-inch cast-iron skillet over medium heat 2 minutes or until hot; melt 2 Tbsp. butter in hot skillet until it begins to foam. Add 4 crab cakes, and cook 3-4 minutes on each side or until browned, reducing heat to medium-low as needed. Transfer to a plate, and keep warm. Repeat procedure with remaining butter and crab cakes. Serve with rémoulade.

CAPER RÉMOULADE

1 cup mayonnaise
1 large garlic clove, finely minced
1 Tbsp. coarsely chopped capers
1 Tbsp. Creole mustard
2 tsp. fresh lemon juice
1 tsp. Worcestershire sauce
½ tsp. Creole seasoning
¼ tsp. hot sauce

CRAB CAKES

1 lb. fresh lump blue crabmeat
2 garlic cloves, finely minced
1 egg yolk
½ cup soft, fresh breadcrumbs
3 Tbsp. mayonnaise
2 Tbsp. finely chopped red bell pepper
1 Tbsp. finely chopped fresh chives
1 tsp. kosher salt
1 tsp. lemon zest
1 tsp. Creole or whole grain mustard
1 tsp. fresh lemon juice
½ tsp. freshly ground black pepper
Dash of hot sauce
¼ cup unsalted butter

Ashley's Grilled Barbecue Chicken Flatbread

One thing is certain: My sister knows how to have a good time! When it comes to food, she's always creating fun and tasty appetizers to get the meal—and party—started. With a glass of wine in hand, she can easily manage herself in the kitchen, at the grill, or as the perfect hostess. Her grilled flatbread is the perfect appetizer for entertaining as it cooks up quickly and can be cut into individual portions to serve by hand.

HANDS-ON 12 MIN. TOTAL **20 MIN.**

MAKES **9** APPETIZERS

1 Preheat grill to 275°-300° (medium-low). Place dough on a baking sheet or cutting board, and drizzle with oil. Stretch or roll dough to ¼-inch thickness, forming a 12- to 13-inch oval.

2 Slide dough from baking sheet onto cooking grate of grill. Grill, covered with grill lid, 3 minutes or until top of dough begins to bubble and grill marks appear on underside. Turn dough over, and reduce grill temperature to 250°-300° (low). Spread barbecue sauce over crust. Top with chicken and next 4 ingredients. Grill, covered with grill lid, 4 minutes or until cheeses melt.

3 Sprinkle with cilantro and salt. Cut into 4-inch squares.

INGREDIENTS

1 lb. bakery pizza dough, at room temperature
1 Tbsp. extra virgin olive oil
1 cup bottled barbecue sauce
2 cups shredded deli-roasted chicken
¼ cup cooked and crumbled bacon
1 cup (4 oz.) shredded Monterey Jack cheese
1 cup (4 oz.) shredded Gouda cheese
½ cup very thin red onion slices
¼ cup loosely packed chopped fresh cilantro
Pinch of kosher salt

My Big Sister

Growing up, I was the "annoying little brother" to my sister, Ashley, poking and prying into her affairs while admiring her friends. Since I was always starting a new school as she was graduating—we are 4 years apart—we never got to share friends or experiences. So upon her graduation from the University of Georgia and mine from high school, my parents did the unthinkable...they sent us on a trip out West. It turned into one of the best trips of my life. I discovered that my sister was one cool chick. She wasn't worried about shopping or going out to fancy restaurants—instead she was content to spend our days fly-fishing and at night listening to live bluegrass. We wandered about Wyoming and Montana, catching rainbows and browns, creating memories that we reminisce about today.

Pulled Pork Barbecue Nachos

Super-indulgent with a Southern, barbecue-infused twist, this play on nachos is always a favorite—not to mention something I crave around 2 a.m. after a night of hitting up the honky-tonks on lower Broadway in Nashville.

That being said, I have a pet peeve when it comes to nachos. You know what I'm talking about. We've all been at the table getting chips without toppings because someone else in the group skims right off the top, stealing all the good stuff. Seriously, don't ever be that guy! To avoid such a social conundrum, I like to layer my chips and ingredients to ensure that each bite is a "perfect bite." Good nacho eating etiquette also demands no double-dipping.

HANDS-ON 19 MIN. **TOTAL 19 MIN.**

SERVES 8-10

INGREDIENTS

2 Tbsp. unsalted butter

2 Tbsp. all-purpose flour

2 cups milk

½ tsp. kosher salt

3 cups (12 oz.) shredded Monterey Jack cheese

1 lb. smoked pulled pork

1 cup bottled vinegar-based barbecue sauce

1 (15-oz.) can black beans, drained and rinsed

1 (12-oz.) bag blue corn tortilla chips

3 plum tomatoes, seeded and diced

¼ cup finely chopped fresh cilantro

½ cup sour cream

½ cup guacamole

¼ cup pickled sliced jalapeño peppers

1 Melt butter in a medium saucepan over medium heat; whisk in flour until smooth. Cook, whisking constantly, 1 minute. Gradually whisk in milk; cook, whisking constantly, until mixture is thickened and bubbly. (Be careful not to scorch milk.) Stir in salt. Remove from heat, and stir in cheese until blended and smooth; keep warm.

2 Combine pork and barbecue sauce in a medium saucepan. Cook over medium heat, stirring occasionally, 2-3 minutes or until thoroughly heated; keep warm. Cook beans in a small saucepan over medium heat, stirring occasionally, 2-3 minutes or until thoroughly heated; keep warm.

3 Arrange half of chips in a single layer on a large serving tray. Layer with half each of beans, pork mixture, tomato, and cilantro. Drizzle with 1 cup cheese sauce. Repeat layers with remaining chips, beans, pork mixture, tomato, and cilantro. Drizzle with 1 cup cheese sauce. Top with sour cream, guacamole, and jalapeño peppers. Serve with remaining 1 cup cheese sauce.

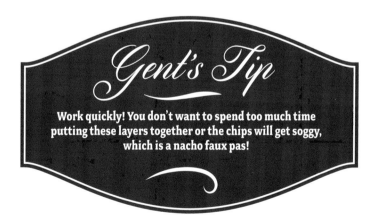

Gent's Tip

Work quickly! You don't want to spend too much time putting these layers together or the chips will get soggy, which is a nacho faux pas!

GREENS + SOUPS + GUMBOS

Simply Southern Salad Dressings

Most folks are intimidated by the thought of creating their own salad dressings. Trust me, your guests will always prefer a homemade salad dressing over the processed concoctions you can buy at the store. I love making dressings to accompany the herbs, fruits, and greens that grow in our beloved region. I make up big batches in Mason jars and store them in the fridge to use throughout the week. Here are some of my favorite dressings to get you started.

Fresh Herb Vinaigrette

HANDS-ON **10 MIN.** TOTAL **15 MIN.**
MAKES **1¼ CUPS**

⇒ INGREDIENTS ⇐

1 garlic clove, minced
1 shallot, finely chopped
¼ cup red wine vinegar
1 Tbsp. Dijon mustard
1 tsp. honey
¾ cup extra virgin olive oil
½ tsp. kosher salt
½ tsp. freshly ground black pepper
1 Tbsp. finely chopped fresh chives
1 Tbsp. finely chopped fresh basil
1 tsp. finely chopped fresh tarragon

1 Combine first 3 ingredients in a glass canning jar, and let stand for 5 minutes.

2 Add mustard and remaining ingredients to vinegar mixture in jar. Cover with metal lid, and screw on band; shake vigorously until blended. Serve immediately or refrigerate up to 1 week.

Bacon + Gorgonzola Balsamic Vinaigrette

HANDS-ON **12 MIN.** TOTAL **12 MIN.**
MAKES **1¾ CUPS**

⇒ INGREDIENTS ⇐

1 shallot, finely chopped
⅓ cup balsamic vinegar
5 thick hickory-smoked bacon slices
1 tsp. Dijon mustard
1 tsp. pure maple syrup
1 tsp. honey
¾ cup extra virgin olive oil
½ tsp. kosher salt
½ tsp. freshly ground black pepper
¼ cup crumbled Gorgonzola cheese
1 Tbsp. finely chopped fresh chives

1 Combine shallot and vinegar in a glass canning jar, and let stand for 5 minutes.

2 Meanwhile, cook bacon in a large skillet over medium-high heat 5-7 minutes or until crisp. Remove bacon, and drain on paper towels, reserving 2 Tbsp. drippings. Crumble bacon.

3 Add crumbled bacon, reserved drippings, Dijon mustard, and remaining ingredients to vinegar mixture in jar. Cover with metal lid, and screw on band; shake vigorously until blended. Serve immediately or refrigerate up to 1 week.

Note: Tested with Benton's Hickory Smoked Country Bacon.

Creamy Buttermilk Dressing

HANDS-ON **10 MIN.** TOTAL **10 MIN.**
MAKES **2 CUPS**

1 Grate zest from lemon to equal ½ tsp. Cut lemon in half; squeeze juice from lemon to equal 2 Tbsp.

2 Whisk together buttermilk and yogurt in a bowl until blended and smooth. Add lemon zest and juice, garlic, salt, pepper, and chives; whisk until blended. Transfer to a glass canning jar, and serve immediately. Cover with metal lid, and screw on band; refrigerate up to 1 week.

≥ INGREDIENTS ≤

1 lemon
½ cup buttermilk
1½ cups plain Greek yogurt
1 garlic clove, minced
1 tsp. kosher salt
1 tsp. freshly ground black pepper
2 Tbsp. finely chopped fresh chives

Classic Caesar Dressing

HANDS-ON **9 MIN.** TOTAL **9 MIN.**
MAKES **1 CUP**

1 Place first 3 ingredients on a cutting board. Using flat side of a chef's knife, carefully smash ingredients together until mixture becomes a thick paste and is thoroughly blended. Transfer paste to a small bowl.

2 Add egg yolks, lemon juice, and vinegar to the paste, and whisk until blended. Add oil in a slow, steady stream, whisking constantly until smooth.

3 Whisk in cheese, and season with black pepper to taste. Transfer to a glass canning jar, and serve immediately. Cover with metal lid, and screw on band; refrigerate up to 1 week.

≥ INGREDIENTS ≤

½ tsp. kosher salt
2 garlic cloves, minced
4 anchovy fillets, minced
2 large pasteurized egg yolks
3 Tbsp. fresh lemon juice
½ tsp. balsamic vinegar
½ cup extra virgin olive oil
¼ cup (1 oz.) freshly grated Parmigiano-
    Reggiano cheese
Freshly ground black pepper

Chopped Seafood Cobb Salad

My taste buds are always hankering for fresh seafood. That's why this salad—especially with all its lean, fresh protein and healthy greens—is one of my all-time favorites when it comes to eating salad for supper. It's also amazing to me how different textures can completely transform a dish—which is the case in this "chopped" salad. By cutting everything into bite-size pieces, you are able to literally get "perfect bites," combining all the great flavors of this dish into every bite. Most deli and seafood counters offer these ingredients precooked, making it a super convenient and easy dish. But if yours doesn't, ask your fishmonger to steam up some of the following ingredients while you shop for the other items you need. This meal is all about working smarter and healthier, not harder.

HANDS-ON **12 MIN.** TOTAL **12 MIN.**

SERVES **6**

⋛ INGREDIENTS ⋚

¾ cup extra virgin olive oil
¼ cup balsamic vinegar
1 Tbsp. whole grain mustard
¾ tsp. kosher salt
½ tsp. freshly ground black pepper
12 oz. bay scallops
½ lb. fresh jumbo lump crabmeat
1 head iceberg lettuce, chopped into bite-size pieces
3 plum tomatoes, finely diced
¼ cup finely diced red onion
3 hard-cooked eggs, diced
4 cooked hickory-smoked bacon slices, crumbled
½ cup crumbled blue cheese
1 lb. peeled, medium-sized cooked shrimp, cut in half lengthwise

1 Whisk together first 5 ingredients in a small bowl until well blended and smooth.

2 Sauté scallops in a lightly greased skillet over medium-high heat 2-3 minutes or until desired degree of doneness. Pick crabmeat, removing any bits of shell. Layer lettuce and next 6 ingredients in order listed in a large serving bowl. Top with scallops and crabmeat. Drizzle three-fourths of olive oil mixture over salad, and toss gently to coat. Add more olive oil mixture, if desired; toss and serve immediately.

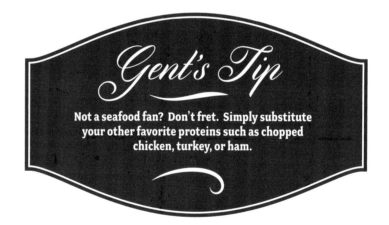

Gent's Tip

Not a seafood fan? Don't fret. Simply substitute your other favorite proteins such as chopped chicken, turkey, or ham.

Green Beans with Cherry Tomatoes + Feta

A light, refreshing salad with plenty of contrasting flavors and colors, this is always a favorite when I serve it at my lake house in Greensboro, Georgia. I find that this dish stands up great on its own, and it also pairs perfectly with any meat coming hot off the grill. If time is of the essence, you can prep the green beans a day in advance and keep them covered in the fridge. Quickly assemble, dress, and serve. Simple. Easy. Beautiful.

HANDS-ON **11 MIN.** TOTAL **16 MIN.**

SERVES **2**

1 Cook haricots verts with ¼ tsp. kosher salt in boiling water to cover in a medium stockpot over high heat 45 seconds to 1 minute or until crisp-tender; drain. Plunge into ice water to stop the cooking process. Let stand 5 minutes or until completely cool. Drain.

2 Pat beans dry with paper towels, and place on a serving plate. Top with cherry tomatoes and crumbled feta. Whisk together oil, next 3 ingredients, remaining ¼ tsp. kosher salt, and desired amount of black pepper until blended and smooth. Drizzle over salad, toss gently, and serve immediately.

⇒ INGREDIENTS ⇐

2 (8-oz.) packages haricots verts (thin green beans), trimmed
½ tsp. kosher salt, divided
1 cup cherry tomatoes, halved
¼ cup crumbled feta cheese
6 Tbsp. extra virgin olive oil
2 Tbsp. Champagne vinegar
½ shallot, minced
½ tsp. Dijon mustard
Freshly ground black pepper

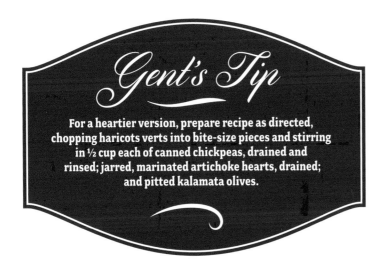

Gent's Tip

For a heartier version, prepare recipe as directed, chopping haricots verts into bite-size pieces and stirring in ½ cup each of canned chickpeas, drained and rinsed; jarred, marinated artichoke hearts, drained; and pitted kalamata olives.

Watermelon + Arugula Salad

Sure, these ingredients might sound like an odd combination, but trust me—put this salad together, and it will be as harmonious as a Coca-Cola with Jack Daniels and peanuts. One of the great things about this dish is its varied colors, textures, and temperatures—it's a roller coaster for the palate. Usually I serve salads family style in a large bowl to allow everyone to dig in, but in this instance, I take some time to put each plate together carefully—to impress my guests with both presentation and great flavors.

HANDS-ON 11 MIN. **TOTAL 1 HR., 11 MIN.**

SERVES 4

→ INGREDIENTS ←

1 large red onion, very thinly sliced (2 cups)
½ cup red wine vinegar
1 Tbsp. sugar
½ tsp. kosher salt
¾ cup balsamic vinegar
4 (1-inch-thick) fresh watermelon slices, rinds removed
1 cup loosely packed arugula
2 oz. crumbled goat cheese

1 Combine first 4 ingredients in a large bowl, stirring to combine; let stand at room temperature 1 hour. (Mixture can be made ahead, and refrigerated in an airtight container up to 1 week.)

2 Heat a small saucepan over medium heat 1 minute or until hot. Add vinegar, bring to a simmer, and cook 5 minutes or until vinegar is reduced to ¼ cup and coats the back of a spoon. Remove from heat. (Vinegar can be prepared up to 1 day ahead.)

3 Cut each watermelon slice into a 4-inch square. Place watermelon squares on individual plates; top with arugula. Drain onion slices, discarding marinade. Arrange ½ cup onion slices over arugula on each salad; sprinkle with goat cheese. Drizzle with reduced balsamic vinegar, and serve immediately.

Grilled Caesar Salad + Sun-dried Tomatoes + Fried Capers

Grilling a salad might sound counterintuitive, but it adds a whole new flavor experience. Developing a nice char on the outside of the romaine not only enhances the presentation, but it also adds a nice depth of smoky flavor. Instead of using croutons, I pan-fry capers, which add a salty, nutty crunch. Without letting anything go to waste, I also fry the capers in the reserved oil from the jarred sun-dried tomatoes, which lends a honeyed flavor to the capers. Of course, the sun-dried tomatoes bring a pop of color and sweetness to help round out the dish.

HANDS-ON **18 MIN.** TOTAL **27 MIN.**

SERVES **4**

1 Preheat grill to 300°-350° (medium).

2 Drain tomatoes, reserving oil and tomatoes separately. Heat reserved oil in a small nonstick skillet over medium-high heat just until oil begins to smoke. Add capers, and fry, gently shaking skillet occasionally, 3-4 minutes or until capers are crispy and browned. Drain capers on paper towels, reserving oil. Let oil cool 15-20 minutes.

3 Brush cut sides of lettuce with cooled reserved oil. Grill lettuce, cut sides down, 2 minutes. Rotate lettuce 45°, and grill on same side 2 more minutes to create grill marks. Place lettuce on serving plates, grilled sides up.

4 Drizzle lettuce with desired amount of dressing. Sprinkle with tomatoes, fried capers, and shaved cheese; season with black pepper to taste. Serve immediately.

⇒ INGREDIENTS ⇐

1 (8.5-oz.) jar sun-dried julienne-cut tomatoes in olive oil

2 tsp. capers, drained and rinsed

2 romaine lettuce hearts, trimmed and cut in half lengthwise

Classic Caesar Dressing (page 53)

2 oz. (½ cup) freshly shaved Parmigiano-Reggiano cheese

Freshly ground black pepper

Georgia Peach Caprese Salad + Balsamic Reduction

This is my play on a traditional Italian Caprese salad—I sub fresh Georgia peaches for vine-ripened tomatoes. From there, I keep it quite simple, using creamy fresh mozzarella cheese and sweet basil to play off the natural sweetness and acidity in the peaches. To set things over the top, I like to reduce some good-quality balsamic vinegar to add gooey, tart, sweet flavor. One tip, however, is to open a window or prepare the balsamic reduction a few hours ahead of hosting any guests—the vinegar smell can remain strong for some time in a poorly ventilated kitchen. Serve this salad on a large platter and pass around the table to share in old Southern style. Please do, however, pass to the right!

HANDS-ON 10 MIN. **TOTAL 15 MIN.**

SERVES 4

1 Heat a small saucepan over medium heat 1 minute or until hot. Add vinegar, bring to a simmer, and cook 5 minutes or until vinegar is reduced to ¼ cup and coats the back of a spoon. Remove from heat. (Vinegar can be prepared up to 1 day ahead.)

2 Alternate peach and mozzarella slices on a large serving platter. Stack basil leaves, and roll up tightly beginning at 1 long side; cut basil crosswise into thin strips or, if using small leaves, leave whole. Arrange basil over peach and mozzarella slices.

3 Drizzle desired amount of reduced balsamic vinegar over salad, reserving remaining balsamic vinegar for another use; refrigerate in an airtight container up to 1 week. Serve salad immediately.

⇒ INGREDIENTS ⇐

¾ cup aged balsamic vinegar

4 fresh, ripe peaches, cut into ¼-inch slices (about 1½ lb. or 2½ cups sliced)

12 oz. fresh mozzarella cheese, cut into ¼-inch slices

¼ cup loosely packed fresh basil leaves

Georgia + Peaches

Mama's family lived a half-day's drive from our house outside Atlanta. South of Macon, we would begin to look for the handwritten signs for fresh peaches, and often we'd pull over to buy juicy, ripe peaches from families peddling them. Biting into a fresh Georgia peach is one of life's true pleasures. I believe the Allman Brothers, of Macon fame, were on to something when they named their famous album *Eat a Peach.* It reminds us to slow down, savor life's moments, and find a bit of joy in nature's creation.

Roasted Gulf Shrimp + Orzo Pasta Salad

This is a nice all-in-one meal that stars tender, sweet Gulf shrimp. I like to go Mediterranean style with my version, using rice-shaped orzo pasta along with traditional ingredients inspired from the region. The key is to not overcook your shrimp! I assure you that my recipe for roasting the shrimp is foolproof—it tastes fantastic every time. I enjoy this dish as a quick lunch (a great combo of lean protein and carbs) and as a side to a summer cookout. As an added bonus, it keeps well for a few days when refrigerated in an airtight container.

HANDS-ON 20 MIN. **TOTAL 55 MIN.**

SERVES 4

≳ INGREDIENTS ≲

- 1½ cups uncooked orzo pasta
- 1 lb. unpeeled, medium-size raw Gulf shrimp
- 6 Tbsp. extra virgin olive oil, divided
- ¼ cup finely diced red onion
- ½ cup seeded, finely diced cucumber
- 1 cup small cherry tomatoes, cut in half
- ¼ cup crumbled feta cheese
- 1 tsp. kosher salt
- ½ tsp. freshly ground black pepper
- 2 Tbsp. fresh lemon juice
- ¼ cup finely chopped fresh parsley

1 Preheat oven to 400°. Cook orzo in a large saucepan in boiling salted water to cover over high heat 6-7 minutes or until al dente. Drain and cool to room temperature.

2 Peel shrimp; devein, if desired. Place shrimp in a single layer in a shallow baking pan, and drizzle with 2 Tbsp. oil. Bake at 400° for 6 minutes or until shrimp turns pink and opaque. Remove from oven; cool to room temperature.

3 Combine orzo, shrimp, remaining 4 Tbsp. olive oil, onion, and remaining ingredients in a large bowl, toss gently until thoroughly blended. Serve immediately, or cover and chill until ready to serve.

Shepherd's Salad

Perfecting this dish is all about the textures. Make sure you dice everything, except the onions, into nice chunky bite-size pieces. That way, they will hold their shape and maintain their natural flavors while allowing the oil and dressing to impart their goodness. This salad makes a simple side dish at summer cookouts when vine-ripe tomatoes are at their peak. Of course, you could serve it alongside a grilled chicken breast for a light supper. Pair this with lighter reds such as pinot noirs, go big with Lebanese wines, or serve it with oaky California chardonnays.

HANDS-ON 10 MIN. **TOTAL 10 MIN.**

SERVES 6

1 Layer first 5 ingredients in a large serving bowl.

2 Whisk together oil and next 3 ingredients in a small bowl until blended. Pour desired amount of dressing over vegetables, and toss gently until coated and blended, being careful not to break apart ingredients. Serve immediately with any remaining dressing.

⇒ INGREDIENTS ⇐

6 tomatoes, cut into bite-size chunks (about 2 lb.)

1 medium English cucumber, cut into bite-size chunks

1 (8-oz.) block feta cheese, cut into bite-size pieces

½ medium red onion, very thinly sliced

1 Tbsp. chopped fresh oregano

½ cup extra virgin olive oil

3 Tbsp. red wine vinegar

1 tsp. kosher salt

½ tsp. freshly ground black pepper

GEORGIA OLIVE FARMS

I'm proud to say that some of the best olive oil in the world comes from the South. Admittedly, that sounds a bit strange as olive harvests have not existed east of the Mississippi since the 1800s. But that all changed when Jason Shaw and his band of brothers introduced Georgia Olive Farms (see page 278). The Shaw family is proving that the sandy soil and hot Georgia climate produce some of the world's most vibrant, rich oils. In fact, many peach and pecan farmers are planting olive orchards so they can harvest this liquid gold. Because the quality of this oil is so darn good, I showcase it in a dish with fresh ingredients where it can really shine.

Mama's Chicken Salad

This recipe, like many in the book, is about keeping things as simple as possible. You'll find other chicken salad recipes with grapes, pecans, and a whole slew of other ingredients... but that ain't the point! Let the chicken shine! The key to perfecting this dish is getting the texture just right—not too chunky, not too processed. I suggest using the back of a fork to slightly mash everything together until just combined. I have laid out Mama's preferred preparation method below, but feel free to use any leftover chicken (grilled, rotisserie, baked, or broiled) you have on hand.

HANDS-ON **20 MIN.** TOTAL **1 HR.**

SERVES **6**

INGREDIENTS

4 large skin-on, bone-in chicken breasts
(about 5 lb.)
4 celery ribs, finely chopped
1 medium Vidalia or sweet onion,
finely chopped
1¼ cups mayonnaise
1 Tbsp. kosher salt
½ Tbsp. freshly ground black pepper

1 Bring chicken breasts and water to cover to a rolling boil in a Dutch oven over medium-high heat. Reduce heat to medium, and cook 20 minutes. Remove from heat, cover, and let stand 30 minutes.

2 Drain chicken, reserving broth for another use. Skin and bone chicken; cut chicken into bite-size pieces. Keep warm.

3 Combine celery and next 4 ingredients in a large bowl. Add chopped chicken, and lightly mash with back of a fork until blended, allowing some chunks to remain. Serve immediately, or refrigerate in an airtight container up to 5 days.

Gent's Tip

**Reserve and freeze the cooking liquid
to use as chicken broth in future recipes.**

Mama's TLC

I'm quite certain that there is no better chicken salad on the planet than my mama's. In fact, I believe world peace might be achieved if those angry fellas and ladies would just sit down for a bite of this delicious masterpiece.

As kids, my sister and I learned early on at the school lunch table that Mama put a bit of extra love into our sack lunches—while most kids were eating overly processed cold cuts, Ashley and I dug into delicious chicken salad sandwiches made from scratch. Sure we were spoiled, but that's what love and great cooking are all about!

Southern Potato Salad

Throughout the South, covered dish dinners are a common theme at cookouts, events, and church-related occasions. Mama used to whip up a big batch of this to share—so did a lot of others. There were often 5-10 dishes of potato salad out on the table. Guess whose always returned empty? Yeah, you got that right.

The key to making this dish perfect is to not overcook the potatoes; otherwise it will turn into mush. It's also important to put it all together while the potatoes are still warm as the heat from the potatoes melds the flavors. In fact, I like this potato dish best when it is still slightly warm. You can substitute plain Greek yogurt for mayonnaise, if you wish.

HANDS-ON 15 MIN. TOTAL 30 MIN.

SERVES 6-8

1 Bring potatoes, 1 tsp. salt, and water to cover to a boil in a Dutch oven over high heat; cook 8 minutes or just until tender. Drain.

2 Place onion in bottom of a large serving bowl. Top with warm potatoes, and let stand 5 minutes.

3 Top with olives, next 5 ingredients, and remaining 1 tsp. kosher salt; toss gently until blended, being careful not to break apart potatoes. Serve immediately, or cover and chill until ready to serve.

⇒ INGREDIENTS ⇐

3 lb. small red potatoes, cut into
  1-inch pieces
2 tsp. kosher salt, divided
½ large Vidalia or sweet onion,
  finely diced (about 1¼ cups)
¼ cup sliced Spanish olives
2 hard-cooked eggs, finely diced
½ cup chopped fresh parsley
1 cup mayonnaise
1 Tbsp. yellow mustard
1 tsp. freshly ground black pepper

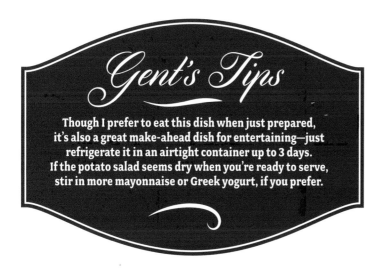

Gent's Tips

Though I prefer to eat this dish when just prepared, it's also a great make-ahead dish for entertaining—just refrigerate it in an airtight container up to 3 days. If the potato salad seems dry when you're ready to serve, stir in more mayonnaise or Greek yogurt, if you prefer.

Not My Sitty's Tabbouleh

As a kid, I was never a big fan of tabbouleh. I can still remember the bitter parsley, grainy bulgur wheat, and sour lemon dressing that seemed to be served at every family occasion. It just didn't do it for me—no matter how much my Mama and the rest of the family seemed to praise it. Fortunately a bit of maturity was all it took to transform my taste buds.

Today, I like to sub quinoa for the bulgur wheat in my Sitty's recipe. For those who might be unfamiliar with quinoa, it boasts a low caloric content and glycemic index rating, yet it's very high in protein and is my grain of choice when I'm craving carbs without the moral hangover. From there, I like to keep everything very simple, straightforward, and classic. I find that it's best to prepare this dish an hour or so in advance— the extra "sitting" time really allows the flavors to improve. In fact, I think it's best when served the day after it's prepared.

HANDS-ON **17 MIN.** TOTAL **30 MIN.**

SERVES **6**

⋛ INGREDIENTS ⋚

1 cup uncooked quinoa
Pinch of kosher salt
1 tsp. extra virgin olive oil
2 garlic cloves, finely minced
2 cups finely chopped fresh
   flat-leaf parsley
2 plum tomatoes, finely diced
½ cup finely diced red onion
3 Tbsp. fresh lemon juice
   (about 1½ lemons)
3 Tbsp. extra virgin olive oil
1¼ tsp. kosher salt
1 tsp. freshly ground black pepper
Dash of ground allspice
1 Tbsp. finely chopped fresh mint

1 Bring first 3 ingredients and 2 cups water to a boil in a 2-qt. saucepan over medium-high heat, stirring once. Cover, reduce heat to medium-low, and simmer 15 minutes or until liquid is absorbed. Remove from heat, and fluff with a fork. Cool to room temperature (about 20-25 minutes).

2 Stir together cooled quinoa, garlic, and remaining ingredients in a large bowl until blended. Serve immediately, or cover and chill until ready to serve.

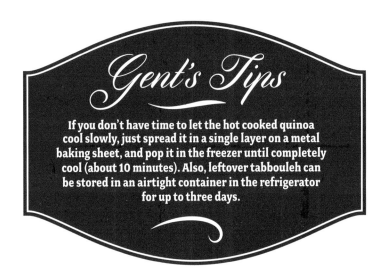

Gent's Tips

If you don't have time to let the hot cooked quinoa cool slowly, just spread it in a single layer on a metal baking sheet, and pop it in the freezer until completely cool (about 10 minutes). Also, leftover tabbouleh can be stored in an airtight container in the refrigerator for up to three days.

Vidalia Onion Soup

If you're going to make this soup, it's important to pronounce the name correctly. So repeat after me, "VI-DALE-YAH Onion Soup." Vidalia, Georgia, is home to this world-famous onion variety, made even more popular by country crooner Sammy Kershaw in his 1996 hit "Vidalia." As the official state vegetable as well as an official trademark owned by the State of Georgia, Vidalias thrive in the rich, low-sulfur soil of southeast Georgia. Praised for their sweet flavor and consistency, these treasured onions start popping up in markets around the country in April and appear throughout the warm growing season.

The natural sugars in Vidalias make them a perfect candidate for my French onion soup. I like to spend a good bit of time caramelizing the onions to develop their sweet, nutty flavor. With the help of some Mississippi beer and good-quality cheese, this is one of my favorite soups to serve when I'm entertaining or to simply enjoy on the couch at home.

HANDS-ON 30 MIN. TOTAL **45 MIN.**

SERVES **6**

1 Tie thyme sprigs into a bundle with kitchen string.

2 Heat a Dutch oven over medium heat 1 minute or until hot; melt butter in Dutch oven. Add onion slices, and stir in salt and pepper. Cook, stirring often, 45 minutes or until onions are caramel colored.

3 Increase heat to medium-high, add thyme bundle and garlic; cook, stirring once or twice, 1 minute or until fragrant. Add ale and sherry, stirring to loosen any browned bits from bottom of Dutch oven. Cook, stirring occasionally, 10 minutes or until liquid is syrupy and thick. Reduce heat to medium, sprinkle flour over onion mixture; cook, stirring occasionally, 3 minutes or until evenly coated, being careful the flour does not burn. Stir in stock, and bring to a light boil; reduce heat to low, and cook 15 minutes. Discard thyme bundle.

4 Preheat broiler with oven rack 5-6 inches from heat. Ladle soup into 6 large broiler-safe bowls, filling each about three-fourths full. Top each with 2 toasted bread slices; sprinkle each with ⅓ cup shredded cheese. Broil 30 seconds-1 minute or until cheese is lightly browned and bubbly. Serve immediately.

Note: Tested with Lazy Magnolia Southern Pecan Nut Brown Ale.

⋛ INGREDIENTS ⋚

3 fresh thyme sprigs
Kitchen string
6 Tbsp. unsalted butter
6 medium Vidalia onions, thinly sliced
1 tsp. kosher salt
1 tsp. freshly ground black pepper
4 garlic cloves, minced
1 cup brown ale
½ cup dry sherry
3 Tbsp. all-purpose flour
6 cups beef stock
12 (½-inch) French baguette slices, lightly toasted
2 cups (8 oz.) shredded Gruyère cheese*

*Swiss cheese may be substituted.

White Bean + Collard Greens Cure-All

Though I love Nashville, I must admit the colder months can be quite depressing—when late fall rolls in and the clocks change, it gets dark at around 4:30 p.m. But, on the bright side, this is one of my favorite seasons for cooking, filled with dark greens, comforting soups, and evenings spent standing over my cast-iron skillet with a hearty red wine or Oktoberfest beer in hand.

This healthy, robust stew is loaded with delicious vegetables, including collards, which are plentiful throughout the season. The best part is that this soup gets cooking in less than 20 minutes, and then it's hands off—making the long evening much more enjoyable by sitting by a warm fire with friends. I suppose that's why this dish cures all of my change-of-season ailments.

HANDS-ON 15 MIN. TOTAL 40 MIN.

MAKES 10½ CUPS

⪥ INGREDIENTS ⪕

1 Tbsp. plus ½ tsp. extra virgin olive oil

1 medium Vidalia or sweet onion, finely diced

3 celery ribs, finely diced

3 carrots, cut into ¼-inch-thick slices

1 tsp. kosher salt

½ tsp. freshly ground black pepper

4 garlic cloves, minced

1 lb. fresh collard greens, washed, trimmed, and finely chopped (about 6 cups)

1 (14.5-oz.) can stewed tomatoes

2 (15-oz.) cans cannellini beans, drained and rinsed

1 qt. chicken stock*

Garnish: freshly shaved Parmigiano-Reggiano cheese

*Vegetable stock may be substituted.

1 Heat a Dutch oven over medium-high heat 1 minute or until hot; add oil. Add onion and next 4 ingredients, and sauté 5 minutes or just until vegetables are tender. Add garlic, and sauté 1 minute. Stir in greens and next 3 ingredients, and bring to a light boil. Cover, reduce heat to low, and simmer 20 minutes.

2 Remove from heat, and serve immediately.

Gent's Tips

With all greens, its important to wash them thoroughly to remove any sand or grit prior to cooking. If you cannot find collard greens, substitute with turnip greens, mustard greens, or kale.

Shrimp + Bacon + Corn "Chowda"

I'm a sucker for warm, hearty chowders. To me, there's no better comfort food to fight back a chilly Southern night. That being said, traditional chowders can be both time-consuming to prepare and overladen with butter and heavy cream. Not this one. I puree the mixture to allow the natural starches in the vegetables to naturally thicken the soup so it requires about half the amount of cream, which really saves on fat and calories. From there, I add just a bit of cheese and cream to comfort the soul. This rustic, weeknight-friendly meal doesn't take too much time to prepare. Lighter and quicker, without any sacrifice in flavor—that's always a winner in my book.

HANDS-ON 40 MIN. TOTAL **1 HR., 25 MIN.,** INCLUDING QUICK SHRIMP STOCK
MAKES 10½ CUPS

1 Peel shrimp, and devein, if desired, reserving shells for Quick Shrimp Stock. Prepare Quick Shrimp Stock.

2 Cut kernels from cobs, discarding cobs. Heat a Dutch oven over medium-high heat 1 minute or until hot. Add bacon, and sauté 4 minutes. Add onion, celery, and corn kernels; sauté 4 more minutes. Add potatoes and garlic; sauté 4 more minutes.

3 Stir in Quick Shrimp Stock, and bring to a light boil. Cover, reduce heat to medium-low, and simmer 8 minutes. Transfer half of mixture to blender. Remove center piece of blender lid (to allow steam to escape); secure blender lid on blender. Place a clean towel over opening in blender lid (to avoid splatters). Puree 10 seconds, leaving mixture chunky. Return processed mixture to Dutch oven.

4 Stir in shrimp, cheese, and whipping cream, and cook, stirring occasionally, 4 minutes or just until shrimp turn pink and cheese is melted and smooth. Remove from heat, and let stand 10 minutes. Stir in chives, salt, and pepper. Serve immediately.

Note: Soup can be processed with a handheld immersion blender on low setting. Be careful not to over process soup—leave a chunky, rustic texture.

⇒ INGREDIENTS ⇐

2 lb. unpeeled, medium-size raw shrimp

4 cups Quick Shrimp Stock*

2 ears sweet yellow corn

4 center-cut bacon slices, diced

1 medium Vidalia or sweet onion, finely diced

3 celery ribs, finely diced

2 large unpeeled russet potatoes, finely diced

3 garlic cloves, minced

1 cup (4 oz.) shredded Monterey Jack cheese

1 cup heavy whipping cream

2 Tbsp. finely chopped chives

½ tsp. kosher salt

1 tsp. freshly ground black pepper

*4 cups reduced-sodium chicken stock may be substituted.

Quick Shrimp Stock

HANDS-ON 15 MIN. TOTAL **25 MIN.**
MAKES 4 CUPS

1 Combine all ingredients and 4 cups water in a Dutch oven. Bring to a boil over medium-high heat. Remove from heat, cover, and let stand 5 minutes.

2 Pour mixture through a wire-mesh strainer into a large bowl, discarding shrimp shells, peppercorns, and bay leaf. Use stock immediately, or freeze in an airtight container up to 3 months.

⇒ INGREDIENTS ⇐

Reserved shrimp shells

½ tsp. kosher salt

4 whole peppercorns

1 bay leaf

Game-Day Venison Chili

Surrounded by plenty of cold beer, college football, and friends—I can honestly say that I'm in paradise when I'm eating a bowl of warm venison chili. If you don't have a freezer full of venison, don't fret! You can simply sub lean ground beef, turkey, or even bison, which can be found at major supermarkets. I like to make up a big pot of this chili to share; refrigerate any leftovers in an airtight container, and heat them up for a tasty lunch on a busy workday. This recipe is delicious served with Fat Bottom American Ale, brewed in Nashville.

HANDS-ON 30 MIN. TOTAL 1 HR.

SERVES 8-10

⇒ INGREDIENTS ⇐

2 Tbsp. extra virgin olive oil

1 large Vidalia or sweet onion,
  finely diced (about 2 cups)

1 green bell pepper,
  finely diced (about 1½ cups)

4 garlic cloves, minced

2 jalapeño peppers, seeded
  and finely diced

2 lb. ground venison

3 Tbsp. chili powder

2 Tbsp. plus 1½ tsp. ground cumin

1 Tbsp. kosher salt

1 tsp. freshly ground black pepper

1 cup amber beer

1 (28-oz.) can tomato sauce

1 (28-oz.) can petite diced tomatoes

1 (14-oz.) can dark red kidney beans,
  drained and rinsed

1 (14-oz.) can black beans,
  drained and rinsed

Toppings: shredded sharp Cheddar
  cheese, sour cream, finely chopped
  green onions

1 Heat a Dutch oven over medium heat 1 minute or until hot; add oil. Add onion and bell pepper; sauté 8 minutes. Add garlic and jalapeño; sauté 2 minutes or just until fragrant.

2 Add venison and next 4 ingredients, and cook, stirring often, 6 minutes or until meat crumbles and is no longer pink. Add beer, and cook, stirring with a wooden spoon to loosen any browned bits from bottom of Dutch oven, 2 minutes.

3 Stir in tomato sauce and next 3 ingredients; reduce heat to medium-low, and simmer, partially covered and stirring occasionally, 30 minutes. Remove from heat, and serve with desired toppings.

Note: Tested with Dos Equis Amber.

Callie's White Bean Chicken Chili

I often get asked what I would eat for my last meal. Truthfully I respond that I feel like I've already eaten mine! Though my wife, Callie, allows me to do most of the cooking, she's no slouch in the kitchen. This recipe, a hand-me-down from her grandma Elly is my all-time favorite.

In addition to being an amazing blend of flavors, this chili is always my go-to request when life and schedules become too hectic. So if, like me, you feel like you've bitten off more than you can chew, slow down and relax a bit by enjoying this deliciously simple recipe.

HANDS-ON 25 MIN. TOTAL **35 MIN.**

SERVES **12½ CUPS**

1 Drain and rinse 3 cans of beans. (Do not drain fourth can.)

2 Heat a Dutch oven over medium heat 1-2 minutes or until hot; add oil. Sauté onion in hot oil 5 minutes. Add garlic and next 4 ingredients, and sauté 5 minutes or until onion is tender and slightly browned.

3 Stir in chiles, broth, and drained and undrained beans. Bring to a simmer, and cook 10 minutes. Add chicken and cheese; cook, stirring occasionally, 3 minutes or until cheese melts and chicken is thoroughly heated. Remove from heat.

4 Top each serving with crushed tortilla chips, and serve immediately.

⇒ INGREDIENTS ⇐

- 4 (15-oz.) cans Great Northern Beans, undrained
- 1 Tbsp. canola oil
- 1 large Vidalia or sweet onion, finely diced
- 1 garlic clove, minced
- 1 tsp. kosher salt
- ½ tsp. freshly ground black pepper
- ½ tsp. ground cumin
- ¼ tsp. dried crushed red pepper
- 2 (4-oz.) cans chopped green chiles, undrained
- 2 cups chicken broth
- 4 cups shredded deli-roasted chicken
- 4 cups (16 oz.) shredded Monterey Jack cheese
- Blue corn tortilla chips, crushed
- Garnish: chopped fresh cilantro

My Wife, Callie

In our first year of marriage, I haphazardly decided to train for a marathon. Unlike my prior races, let's just say that my training schedule was less disciplined. Boy, did I pay for it on a humid December day in Huntsville, Alabama. Of course, marathons are never easy—but there's nothing worse than going for 26.2 when you feel winded after a mile. Driving back to Nashville I had to pull over a few times just to prevent from nodding off. Needless to say, I was in bad shape when I got home. Seeing my beautiful wife helped cure some of my aches and pains, but it was a few bowls of her chili that literally resurrected me from my suffering! I will never forget that meal.

Classic Tomato Soup + Goat Cheese + Pecan Crostini

Whenever possible, I like to eat what's fresh and in season. But I'll be damned if that philosophy doesn't always come back to bite me in the butt when I get a hankering for a comforting bowl of tomato soup, as the vine-ripe tomatoes of summer are no longer around. So instead, I rely on canned tomatoes to satisfy my craving. In this case, those canned tomatoes are a good thing. As it turns out, canned and frozen vegetables are picked and processed at the peak of the season and stored for later use throughout the year.

Unlike most tomato soups, I like to start out with a full mirepoix (onion, celery, and carrots) as the base of the dish—I find the extra vegetables add a nice depth of flavor to the final result. Instead of a grilled cheese sandwich, I'm serving up a crispy, cheesy crostini that's nutty in flavor and perfect for sopping up that delicious soup.

HANDS-ON **22 MIN.** TOTAL **54 MIN.**
MAKES **8 CUPS**

INGREDIENTS

1 Tbsp. plus 1½ tsp. extra virgin olive oil
1 medium Vidalia or sweet onion, finely diced
1 carrot, finely diced
2 celery ribs, finely diced
¾ tsp. kosher salt
½ tsp. freshly ground black pepper
¼ tsp. dried crushed red pepper
3 garlic cloves, finely minced
1 bay leaf
1 (28-oz.) can whole peeled tomatoes (preferably San Marzano brand)
2½ cups reduced-sodium chicken broth
½ cup heavy cream
8-10 fresh basil leaves
Goat Cheese & Pecan Crostini

1 Heat a Dutch oven over medium-high heat 1 minute or until hot; add oil. Add onion and next 5 ingredients; sauté 8 minutes. Add garlic and bay leaf, and sauté 1 minute or until fragrant.

2 Add tomatoes, and cook, stirring with a wooden spoon to loosen any browned bits from bottom of Dutch oven and roughly breaking apart tomatoes, 1 minute. Add chicken broth, and bring mixture to a light boil. Partially cover, reduce heat to medium-low, and simmer 10 minutes.

3 Turn off heat; remove and discard bay leaf. Process tomato mixture with a handheld immersion blender until smooth. (Very small bits may remain.) Stir in cream until thoroughly blended. Ladle soup into bowls, and sprinkle with fresh basil. Serve with Goat Cheese & Pecan Crostini.

Goat Cheese + Pecan Crostini

HANDS-ON **15 MIN.** TOTAL **22 MIN.**
SERVES **8**

INGREDIENTS

8 (¼-inch-thick) ciabatta bread slices
2 Tbsp. extra virgin olive oil, divided
¼ cup finely chopped pecans
1 (4-oz.) herbed goat cheese log
Freshly ground black pepper

1 Preheat oven to 400°. Arrange ciabatta slices on a baking sheet, and brush with 1 Tbsp. of oil. Bake for 12 minutes.

2 Meanwhile, heat pecans in a small nonstick skillet over medium-low heat, stirring often, 5 minutes or until toasted and fragrant. Remove from heat.

3 Spread goat cheese over toasted ciabatta slices, and sprinkle with toasted pecans. Drizzle slices with remaining 1 Tbsp. olive oil, and season with freshly ground black pepper to taste.

Lemony Chicken + Rice Soup

I'm a fan of making my own stocks and broths. After all, purchasing those items at the store can get quite expensive. My wife often thinks I'm crazy when I'm stuffing plastic bags full of leftover bones and carcasses, carrot butts and tips, celery hearts, and onion trimmings into our freezer. Well, I put all of that "throwaway" stuff to good use when I'm ready to make stocks and broths.

In this recipe, I slowly braise a whole chicken, which yields both a delicious broth and plenty of cooked meat for the base of this classic soup. I grew up eating quite a bit of chicken and rice soup—it was one of Daddy's favorites. My version is a little different, substituting wild rice for white rice and adding a bit of a spike in the form of fresh lemon juice.

HANDS-ON 25 MIN. **TOTAL 2 HR., 40 MIN.**

MAKES 13½ CUPS

1 Combine first 5 ingredients in a 6-qt. Dutch oven, and add water to cover (about 12 cups). Bring to a boil over medium-high heat. Cover, reduce heat to low, and simmer 1 hour and 15 minutes, skimming foam as needed. Remove chicken, reserving liquid and vegetables in Dutch oven. Cool chicken 30 minutes; skin, bone, and coarsely chop chicken to equal 5 cups. Loosely cover chicken, and chill until ready to use. Meanwhile, pour liquid through a wire-mesh strainer into a large bowl, discarding solids. Skim fat from broth.

2 Return Dutch oven to medium-high heat; add oil. Add onion, celery, and carrot; stir in salt, pepper, and thyme, and sauté 5 minutes or just until vegetables are tender. Add garlic, and sauté 1 minute or just until fragrant. Stir in broth, and bring to a light boil. Stir in rice, and return to a boil. Reduce heat to medium, and cook, covered, 40 minutes or until rice is al dente. Stir in 5 cups chopped cooked chicken and lemon juice. Serve immediately.

≩ INGREDIENTS ≲

1 (3- to 4-lb.) whole chicken, quartered
2 cups fresh or frozen carrot, onion, and celery chunks
10 whole black peppercorns
2 bay leaves
1 Tbsp. kosher salt
1 Tbsp. extra virgin olive oil
1 medium Vidalia or sweet onion, diced
3 celery ribs, cut into ¼-inch slices
3 carrots, cut into ¼-inch slices
1 tsp. kosher salt
1 tsp. freshly ground black pepper
1 tsp. dried thyme
2 garlic cloves, minced
1½ cups uncooked wild rice
3 Tbsp. fresh lemon juice
Garnish: chopped fresh parsley

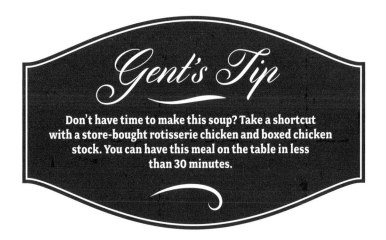

Gent's Tip

Don't have time to make this soup? Take a shortcut with a store-bought rotisserie chicken and boxed chicken stock. You can have this meal on the table in less than 30 minutes.

"Frog Moore" Stew

Mystery and controversy often add a dash of intrigue to Southern cuisine, and clearly that's the case with Frogmore stew, a Lowcountry favorite. This dish is less stew like than the name would leave you to believe—it's usually drained from the boiling liquid entirely. According to some, Richard Gay, owner of Gay Fish Company, coined the famous "frogmore" moniker after the Frogmore community located on South Carolina's St. Helena Island. About half the locals give the naming credit to Gay, while others each sport their own proprietary claims. Moreover, outsiders often believe the dish actually contains frogs, which is certainly not true. Since this dish carries so many distinctions and allegations, I prefer to give it my own spin—adding my last name, to boot. (Why not, right?) Traditionally poured out on newspaper-lined tables for large gatherings, I like to present this dish in servable portions so everyone gets the entire flavor of the Lowcountry in their own bowl. This stew pairs well with crisp lagers or nutty, amber ales. Serve with toasted or grilled bread on the side to round out the meal.

HANDS-ON **43 MIN.** TOTAL **43 MIN.**

SERVES **8**

⇒ INGREDIENTS ⇐

2 Tbsp. olive oil

1 medium Vidalia or sweet onion, chopped

2 garlic cloves, minced

1 bay leaf

¼ cup Old Bay seasoning

½ tsp. freshly ground black pepper

¼ tsp. dried crushed red pepper

1 (14.5-oz.) can petite diced tomatoes, drained

4 cups seafood stock*

1 tsp. kosher salt

2 lb. petite red potatoes, cut in half

4 ears fresh corn, husks removed and broken in half

1 lb. smoked sausage, cut into ½-inch pieces

2 lb. unpeeled, extra-large raw Georgia shrimp

¼ cup unsalted butter

Garnish: fresh chopped parsley

*Reduced-sodium chicken stock may be substituted.

1 Heat a Dutch oven over medium-high heat 1 minute or until hot; add oil. Add onion, and sauté 5 minutes or just until tender. Stir in garlic and next 4 ingredients, and cook, stirring constantly, 1 minute.

2 Add tomatoes, and cook, stirring often, 5 minutes or until tomatoes begin to thicken slightly. Add seafood stock, and cook, stirring with a wooden spoon to loosen any browned bits from bottom of Dutch oven, 1 minute. Stir in salt, and bring mixture to a boil. Add potatoes; cover and cook 10 minutes.

3 Add corn and sausage, and return to a boil; cover and cook 5 minutes. Stir in shrimp, submerging in cooking liquid; cover and cook 3 minutes. Remove Dutch oven from heat, and let stand 8 minutes or just until shrimp turn bright pink and firm. Stir in butter until melted. Remove and discard bay leaf.

4 Spoon potatoes, corn, sausage, and shrimp into 8 shallow bowls using a slotted spoon. Ladle desired amount of cooking liquid into each bowl. Serve immediately.

GEORGIA + SHRIMP

There's no person more knowledgeable about the shrimping industry than Michael Sullivan. Captain of the Flying Cloud, Michael has been shrimping off the Georgia coast since his teens. He's one of the good guys—one that can tell you story after story while sitting on coolers drinking cold beer.

That being said, Michael's way of life, and his industry, needs our attention. Rising fuel costs, cheap low-quality imports from abroad, and a mysterious black gill disease have all but ruined the shrimp harvest in Georgia. When so many are seeking local, high-quality ingredients, now is the time to support this fledgling industry. A wild caught, fresh Georgia shrimp tastes leaps and bounds better than anything imported. Support local and keep Michael out on the water reeling in net after net of nature's bounty.

Gulf Coast Cioppino

Cioppino is a dish that traces its origins to San Francisco, which is quite a long way from Ole Dixie. Nevertheless I like to pay homage by incorporating ingredients that are native to our Southern coastal waters such as quahogs, blue crabs, amberjack, and shrimp.

It's rumored that this dish first got its name from Italian immigrant sea fishermen. After a long day fishing the bay, the men would return to the docks to create a rich hearty stew from the day's catch. Each fisherman was encouraged to "chip in, eh" to make the meal.

The beauty of this dish is that it's based on your day's catch or your own preferences. Sub your preferred seafood to make it entirely your own. I like to serve cioppino with toasted ciabatta or sourdough bread for mopping up the flavorful broth.

HANDS-ON 33 MIN. TOTAL 1 HR., 22 MIN.
MAKES 14½ CUPS

INGREDIENTS

- 2 lb. unpeeled, large raw Gulf shrimp
- ¼ cup extra virgin olive oil
- 1 large Vidalia or sweet onion, finely diced
- 1 tsp. kosher salt
- ½ tsp. freshly ground black pepper
- 4 garlic cloves, minced
- ¼ tsp. dried crushed red pepper
- ¼ cup tomato paste
- 1 (12-oz.) bottle amber beer
- 1 (28-oz.) can whole peeled tomatoes, undrained
- 4 cups seafood stock*
- 2 bay leaves
- 1 lb. littleneck clams, scrubbed
- 8 blue crabs, cleaned and cut in half
- 1½ lb. amberjack fillet, cut into 1½-inch chunks
- Ciabatta or sourdough bread slices, toasted
- Garnish: chopped fresh parsley

*Chicken stock may be substituted.

1 Peel shrimp, leaving tails on; devein shrimp, if desired; set aside. Heat a large Dutch oven over medium heat 1 minute or until hot; add oil. Stir in onion, salt, and pepper; sauté 10 minutes. Add garlic and red pepper; sauté 2 minutes.

2 Push sautéed onion mixture to outer edges of Dutch oven, making a well in center. Add tomato paste to well, and cook until paste is slightly browned; stir tomato paste into onion mixture until thoroughly blended. Add beer, and cook, stirring with a wooden spoon to loosen browned bits from bottom of Dutch oven, 1 minute.

3 Crush tomatoes with juices with clean hands. Add tomatoes, seafood stock, and bay leaves; bring to a boil over medium-high heat, stirring occasionally. Reduce heat to medium-low, and simmer, partially covered, 30 minutes. Add clams, and cook 3-4 minutes or until clams open. (Discard any clams that do not open.) Add reserved peeled shrimp, crabs, and amberjack; cover and cook, stirring occasionally, 6 minutes or just until shrimp and crabs turn pink and fish is firm.

4 Remove from heat; remove and discard bay leaves. Serve in large bowls, dividing seafood and broth evenly. Serve with toasted bread slices.

Note: Tested with San Marzano canned tomatoes.

Brunswick Stew

Though folks in Brunswick County, Virginia, believe they were first to create this dish, I'm here to settle the score. This once squirrel-based stew was proudly created and perfected in Brunswick, Georgia. Well, at least that's my story, and I'm sticking to it.

Brunswick stew is really a necessity in barbecue joints throughout the South. It serves as a "catch-all" stew for any leftover meats such as pork, chicken, beef, or yes, wild game. There are endless variations on how to prepare this dish, along with the ingredients it should contain. My version is much like the one I grew up on, featuring an array of meats and a sweet and spicy tomato base. Since venison is often in my freezer, I usually substitute it for ground beef.

HANDS-ON **42 MIN.** TOTAL **3 HR., 4 MIN.**

MAKES **22 CUPS**

1 Melt butter in an 8-qt. Dutch oven over medium-high heat. Add chicken, and cook 10 minutes or until desired degree of doneness, turning once. Transfer cooked chicken to a plate, reserving drippings in Dutch oven. Add venison to Dutch oven; cook, stirring frequently, 5 minutes or until meat crumbles and is no longer pink. Remove venison with slotted spoon, reserving drippings in Dutch oven. When chicken is cool, shred with 2 forks.

2 Add onion, bell pepper, and celery to reserved drippings in Dutch oven; stir in salt, pepper, and bay leaves. Sauté over medium-high heat 7 minutes or just until vegetables are softened. Add garlic, and sauté 1 minute. Add beer, and cook, stirring with a wooden spoon to loosen any browned bits from bottom of Dutch oven, 1 minute. Stir in tomatoes and next 6 ingredients. Bring to a light boil; cover, reduce heat to low, and simmer, stirring occasionally, 1½ hours.

3 Stir in corn, pork, and cooked chicken and venison. Cover and simmer 30 minutes. Remove from heat; season with salt and pepper to taste, and let stand 10 minutes. Remove and discard bay leaves before serving.

Note: Tested with RCH Old Slug Porter Dark Ale.

INGREDIENTS

½ cup unsalted butter
1¾ lb. skinned and boned chicken thighs
1½ lb. ground venison or lean ground beef
2 medium Vidalia or sweet onions, diced
2 green bell peppers, diced
3 celery ribs, diced
1½ tsp. kosher salt
1 tsp. freshly ground black pepper
2 bay leaves
4 garlic cloves, finely minced
1 cup porter beer
1 (28-oz.) can fire-roasted tomatoes
4 cups chicken stock
1½ cups bottled vinegar-based barbecue sauce
2 Tbsp. light brown sugar
2 Tbsp. Worcestershire sauce
1 Tbsp. hot sauce
1 (16-oz.) package frozen baby lima beans
4 cups fresh corn kernels (about 5 ears)
1 lb. smoked pulled pork

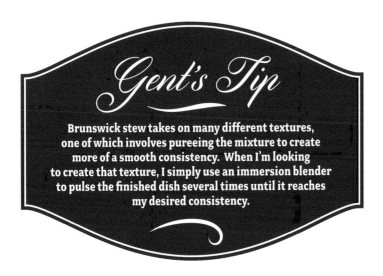

Gent's Tip

Brunswick stew takes on many different textures, one of which involves pureeing the mixture to create more of a smooth consistency. When I'm looking to create that texture, I simply use an immersion blender to pulse the finished dish several times until it reaches my desired consistency.

Seafood Gumbo

Gumbo is my king of all kings when it comes to soaking in the flavor of the Deep South in one bite. I have been honing this recipe for more than 10 years, and I'm proud of the result. In fact, I would challenge any Cajun grandma to come up with a better version. Full disclosure: I add tomatoes to my gumbo—I prefer the rich, acidic bite. I also use okra, therefore I do not finish with filé powder. It's one or the other in my opinion, never both.

The key to perfecting this dish is to be patient when it comes to making the roux. You'll need to keep a close watch on it throughout the cooking process, stirring it constantly over low heat to prevent it from burning. The darker the roux, the better the gumbo. This recipe is the incredibly simple culmination of several regional adaptations that I've worked on throughout the years. Enjoy!

HANDS-ON **1 HR., 50 MIN.** TOTAL **2 HR.**

MAKES **22 CUPS**

⇒ INGREDIENTS ⇐

6 cups seafood stock

1 lb. andouille sausage, cut into
  ¼-inch slices

4 cups fresh sliced okra

1 cup vegetable oil or melted shortening

1 cup all-purpose flour

1 large Vidalia or sweet onion,
  finely diced

1 large bell pepper, finely diced

3 celery ribs, finely diced

1 tsp. kosher salt

1 tsp. freshly ground black pepper

¼ tsp. ground red pepper

½ tsp. Creole seasoning

2 bay leaves

6 garlic cloves, minced

1 (28-oz.) can petite diced
  tomatoes, undrained

1 lb. fresh oysters, undrained

1 lb. fresh lump crabmeat

2 lb. unpeeled, medium-size raw shrimp,
  peeled and deveined

1 (12-oz.) package frozen cooked, peeled
  crawfish tail meat, thawed and drained

Hot cooked white rice

Garnish: thinly sliced green onions

1 Heat seafood stock in a large saucepan over low heat until thoroughly heated. Keep stock warm.

2 Heat a large Dutch oven over medium heat 1 minute or until hot. Add sausage, and cook, stirring occasionally, 5 minutes or until browned; transfer to a plate using a slotted spoon, reserving drippings in Dutch oven. Add okra, and sauté 4 minutes or just until tender; transfer okra to a plate, reserving drippings in Dutch oven.

3 Reduce heat to medium-low; add oil and flour to reserved drippings in Dutch oven. Cook, stirring constantly, until flour is a dark brown peanut butter color (about 25-30 minutes).

4 Stir in onion, bell pepper, and celery. Add salt and next 4 ingredients, increase heat to medium, and sauté 5 minutes. Add garlic, and sauté 3-4 more minutes.

5 Add tomatoes, and cook, stirring to loosen browned bits from bottom of Dutch oven, 1 minute. Add warm stock, 1 cup at a time, stirring constantly, until thoroughly blended. Bring to a light boil, stirring occasionally.

6 Reduce heat to medium-low; cover and simmer, stirring occasionally, 15 minutes. Return cooked sausage and okra to Dutch oven; cover and simmer, stirring occasionally, 20 minutes.

7 Drain oysters, reserving oyster liquor. Stir oysters, reserved liquor, crabmeat, shrimp, and crawfish into sausage mixture, making sure seafood is immersed completely in mixture; cook 2 minutes. Turn off heat; cover and let stand 10 to 15 minutes. Add Creole seasoning to taste; remove and discard bay leaves. Serve gumbo in bowls; top each serving with hot cooked rice.

Venison Gumbo

The beauty of having so many avid hunters as friends is that I receive many gifts throughout the year ranging from wild turkey to deer sausage and elk steaks, depending on the season. Let's just say that I've got a good gig going here in the Music City.

I first created this recipe on a rainy Sunday afternoon while watching the Titans battle it out on the gridiron. My buddy, Miller Gunn—a great name for a hunter—called to inform me about his fresh kill, and he pulled up an hour later with a field-dressed deer in his pickup truck. I immediately went to work on breaking everything down to host friends for a day of football and food. I love preparing the hindquarter, or stew meat, for gumbo as the cut gets super tender after a few hours of braising in the liquid. I choose this rich, hearty stew to serve as an introduction to venison for friends who either have not tried it before or felt it was too gamey. When prepared in this recipe, many guests mistake the venison for beef, which can always be substituted when necessary. This dish pairs well with a rich, nutty porter beer or a full-bodied cabernet sauvignon.

HANDS-ON 1 HR. TOTAL 5 HR.
MAKES 13½ CUPS

1 Bring stock to a simmer in a large saucepan over medium-high heat. Reduce heat to low; gently simmer until ready to use.

2 Heat a large Dutch oven over medium heat 2 minutes or until hot. Add venison, and cook, turning occasionally, 6 minutes or until browned on all sides; transfer venison to a plate using a slotted spoon, reserving drippings in Dutch oven. Add okra to hot drippings, and sauté 4 minutes or just until tender; transfer okra to a plate.

3 Reduce heat to medium-low; add oil and flour to Dutch oven, and cook, whisking constantly, until flour is a dark chocolate color (about 30 minutes).

4 Stir in onion and next 7 ingredients. Increase heat to medium-high, and sauté onion mixture 5 minutes. Add garlic, and sauté 3 minutes.

5 Add tomatoes, and cook, stirring to loosen any browned bits from bottom of Dutch oven, 1 minute. Add warm stock, 1 cup at a time, stirring constantly, until blended after each addition.

6 Bring mixture to a light boil, stirring occasionally. Reduce heat to medium-low; cover and simmer 30 minutes. Return venison to Dutch oven; cover and simmer 3 hours or until venison is very tender.

7 Meanwhile, cut kernels from cobs; discard cobs. Return okra to Dutch oven, and stir in corn kernels. Simmer 30 minutes; remove and discard bay leaves. Spoon into bowls, and top with hot cooked rice; serve immediately.

INGREDIENTS

6 cups beef stock
2 lb. venison hindquarter, cut into 1-inch pieces
1 lb. fresh okra, cut into ½-inch slices (4 cups)
½ cup vegetable oil
½ cup all-purpose flour
1 large Vidalia or sweet onion, finely diced
1 large red bell pepper, finely diced
3 celery ribs, finely diced
2 bay leaves
2 tsp. kosher salt
1 tsp. freshly ground black pepper
½ tsp. Creole seasoning
¼ tsp. ground red pepper
6 garlic cloves, finely minced
1 (28-oz.) can petite diced tomatoes, undrained
4 ears fresh yellow corn, husks removed
Hot cooked white rice
Garnish: thinly sliced green onions

MAIN ATTRACTIONS

Sitty's Fried Chicken

My grandmother Sitty's secret recipe for fried chicken is all about the dredge, which uses basic seasoning, flour, and water. Simplicity is the key—after all, the star of the show is the chicken. Mama said that my grandfather Giddy, who was a butcher by trade, taught Sitty that the best chickens were those that weighed around 3 pounds.

These days, it's almost impossible to find a chicken that size, so opt for a free-range or organic chicken because those birds are usually the perfect size. Preparing the chicken in the following manner will yield a very thin, crisp coating and juicy, tender chicken beneath. Sitty's secret is finally out.

HANDS-ON 35 MIN. TOTAL 1 HR., 35 MIN.

SERVES 4

1 Rinse chicken with cold water, and pat dry. Place chicken in a large bowl; sprinkle with salt and pepper, tossing to coat. Sprinkle flour and ½ cup water over chicken; toss chicken with flour mixture, using fingers to rub flour paste into skin until thoroughly coated. Cover with plastic wrap, and chill 1-24 hours.

2 Pour oil to a depth of 1 inch into a 12-inch cast-iron skillet. Heat oil over medium heat to 350°.

3 Fry drumsticks and thighs in hot oil, bone sides down, 8 minutes. (Increase heat for first few minutes, if necessary, to maintain oil temperature at 350°.) Carefully turn chicken, rotating pieces away from your body; fry 8 more minutes or until browned and desired degree of doneness. Remove chicken, and transfer to a wire rack over paper towels. Repeat procedure with remaining chicken pieces (breasts and wings), reducing frying time to 7 minutes on each side.

Note: Tested with White Lily Enriched Bleached All-Purpose Flour.

═ INGREDIENTS ═

1 (3-lb.) whole chicken, cut into 8 pieces
2 tsp. kosher salt
1 tsp. freshly ground black pepper
1 cup all-purpose flour
Peanut oil

Seasoned With Love

This dish has been a family favorite for decades—in fact, no family event was complete without a basket of fried chicken on the table. I'm happy and humbled to share Sitty's famous recipe so you can create similar memories for your family. Remember one thing Sitty taught me...food is best prepared when seasoned with love.

Sunday Roast Chicken + Roasted Vegetables

Most of my best dinner parties come together casually. It's usually after church on Sunday when my planning begins. I run into friends whom I haven't seen in a while—often due to the fact that they have been busy out on the road promoting their latest albums or business ventures. In Nashville, it's known that the best nights for entertaining are Sunday, Monday, and Tuesday, when the tourists have left. I like to invite folks over for some home cooking with my simple roast chicken and vegetables. Please note, I do charge a convenience fee for such a meal, usually in the form of a bottle of wine and good conversation.

This recipe allows all of the vegetables to soak up the herb and acidic flavors from the chicken drippings—it's absolutely delicious. Paired up with a leafy green salad, some crusty bread, and a simple dessert, this meal exudes casual, yet elegant entertaining.

HANDS-ON 20 MIN. TOTAL **1 HR., 45 MIN.**

SERVES **4**

⇒ INGREDIENTS ⇐

- 1 (5-lb.) whole chicken
- ¼ cup unsalted butter, softened
- 2½ tsp. kosher salt, divided
- 1½ tsp. freshly ground black pepper, divided
- 1 garlic bulb
- 1 lemon, cut in half
- 4 fresh thyme sprigs
- 1 lb. small red potatoes, halved
- 5 carrots, peeled and cut in half crosswise
- 1 medium Vidalia or sweet onions, peeled and quartered
- 2 yellow beets, peeled and quartered
- 1 Tbsp. olive oil

1 Preheat oven to 425°. If applicable, remove giblets from chicken, and reserve for another use. Rinse chicken, and pat dry. Stir together butter, 2 tsp. salt, and 1 tsp. pepper in a bowl until thoroughly blended. Loosen and lift skin from chicken breasts and drumsticks with fingers (do not totally detach skin). Rub butter mixture under skin; replace skin. Cut off pointed end of garlic. Place garlic, lemon halves, and thyme sprigs in chicken cavity.

2 Combine potatoes and next 3 ingredients in a large roasting pan; drizzle with oil, and sprinkle remaining ½ tsp. salt and ½ tsp. pepper. Toss mixture until well coated. Push vegetable mixture to edges of roasting pan; place chicken, breast side up, in center of pan.

3 Bake at 425° for 1 hour and 15 minutes or until a meat thermometer inserted in thigh registers 165°. Remove from oven, cover loosely with aluminum foil, and let stand 10 minutes. Transfer chicken to a cutting board, and cut into individual portions. Serve with roasted vegetables, and drizzle with pan drippings.

My Uncle Al and Aunt Marcia

My intro to cooking television came from sitting on the couch while Al enjoyed an early evening cocktail, and I watched him take notes on a legal pad as he perused cooking shows via public television. He was a "foodie" long before the term existed, and I owe him credit for teaching me how to properly scramble eggs (use butter, cook over a low flame, stir constantly, and finish with cream) and also for giving me my first taste of roasted leg of lamb with mint jelly.

Lemon-Oregano Roasted Chicken + Broiled Feta

My sister Ashley and I were fanatics for feta cheese—a byproduct of Mama's nightly Greek salads—so this dish, inspired by one of my Uncle Al's, was always a useful way to get us out of the same ole chicken dinner routine.

Roasting chicken breasts with the skin on and bone in yields a moist, delicious result every time. The keys to success are using a heavy-bottomed cast-iron pan and allowing the heat to crisp up the skin without moving the chicken about during the searing process.

HANDS-ON 10 MIN. **TOTAL 4 HR., 38 MIN.**

SERVES 4

1 Cut lemons in half. Squeeze juice from lemons into a measuring cup to equal ¼ cup. Smash garlic using flat side of a knife. Combine lemon juice, garlic, oil, and next 3 ingredients in a large zip-top plastic freezer bag; add chicken, turning to coat. Seal bag, and chill 4-24 hours.

2 Preheat oven to 400°. Place a 12-inch cast-iron skillet over medium-high heat 2 minutes or until hot. Remove chicken from marinade, discarding marinade. Cook chicken, skins side down, 3 minutes (to ensure even searing on the skin, do not disturb chicken).

3 Turn chicken over, and transfer skillet to oven. Bake at 400° for 25-30 minutes or until a meat thermometer inserted in thickest portion of breast registers 165°. Remove skillet from oven.

4 Preheat broiler with oven rack 3 inches from heat. Sprinkle chicken with feta. Broil chicken in skillet 2 minutes or until cheese just begins to melt and is lightly browned. Transfer chicken to a platter, and serve immediately.

⋛ INGREDIENTS ⋚

2 lemons
8 garlic cloves
½ cup extra virgin olive oil
¼ cup loosely packed chopped fresh oregano
1½ tsp. kosher salt
3 tsp. freshly ground black pepper
4 skin-on, bone-in chicken breasts
1 (4-oz.) package crumbled feta cheese
Garnish: fresh oregano leaves

Old-School Chicken + Dumplings

Most classic Southern food is hearty and rich due to the fact that the South was founded as an agrarian society. Men and women worked long, hard days tending their crops and livestock. When mealtime came, cooks not only had to make use of what was in season, but also what could sustain and fuel these tireless workers. Chicken and dumplings is one of those quintessential meals. Unlike the puffy dough-ball dumplings beloved by Yanks, true Southern dumplings are rolled out and cut by hand.

My recipe is "old school" in the sense that I focus on the basics—chicken, vegetables, flour, butter, milk, and cream. I prefer to use chicken thighs in this recipe instead of white meat chicken. Not only are the thighs cheaper, but also the skin renders delicious fat while keeping the dark meat nice and moist.

So even though this recipe is made entirely from scratch, it's still something you can have on your table in about an hour.

HANDS-ON 50 MIN. TOTAL **1 HR., 10 MIN.**

SERVES 6

⋛ INGREDIENTS ⋚

2 lb. skin-on, bone-in chicken thighs

1½ tsp. kosher salt, divided

½ tsp. freshly ground black pepper

1 medium Vidalia or sweet onion, finely diced

5 carrots, cut into ½-inch pieces

3 celery ribs, cut into ½-inch pieces

2 garlic cloves, chopped

1 tsp. finely chopped fresh thyme

2 cups heavy cream

2 cups all-purpose flour

3 Tbsp. cold unsalted butter, cut into pieces

1 cup very cold buttermilk

Parchment paper

Garnish: chopped fresh thyme and parsley

1 Place a Dutch oven over medium-high heat 1 minute or until hot. Pat chicken dry, and sprinkle both sides with 1 tsp. salt and ½ tsp. pepper. Cook chicken in hot Dutch oven, skin sides down, 5 minutes on each side. Transfer chicken to a plate, reserving drippings in Dutch oven.

2 Add onion, carrot, and celery to hot drippings, and sauté 6 minutes or just until tender. Add garlic and thyme, and sauté 1 minute or until fragrant. Return chicken and any accumulated juices to vegetable mixture. Stir in 3 cups water and 2 cups cream; bring to a light boil. Cover, reduce heat to low, and simmer 20 minutes.

3 Meanwhile, stir together flour and remaining ½ tsp. salt. Cut butter into flour mixture with a pastry blender or fork until crumbly and mixture resembles small peas. Add buttermilk, stirring just until dry ingredients are moistened. Turn dough out onto a lightly floured surface. Lightly sprinkle flour over top of dough, and knead dough with floured hands 4-6 times or just until dough starts coming together. Using a lightly floured rolling pin, roll dough into a 15- x 12-inch rectangle about ⅛-inch thick. Cut dough into 2-inch vertical strips, and cut strips crosswise every 2 inches, creating 2-inch squares (some will be irregularly shaped). Dust squares with flour, and transfer to a parchment paper–lined baking sheet.

4 Uncover Dutch oven, and transfer chicken to a plate, reserving cream mixture in Dutch oven. Increase heat to medium, and bring mixture to a simmer. Add dumplings, a few at a time, stirring gently. Cook, stirring occasionally, 10 minutes or until dumplings are firm. Meanwhile, skin and bone chicken; tear chicken into bite-size pieces. Return chicken to Dutch oven, and cook, stirring occasionally, 2 minutes or until chicken is thoroughly heated. Let stand 10 minutes before serving.

Gent's Tip

If you have some of the goat cheese mixture left over, spread it on a toasted bagel the next morning, or fold it into a simple egg omelet. Dinner and breakfast perfection—ain't life grand?

Pecan-Crusted Chicken + Peppered Goat Cheese

Sometimes I find myself stuck in a rut when it comes to chicken—grilled, baked, sautéed, roasted, it all starts to taste the same. So instead, I created this meal utilizing some of my favorite ingredients to make an elegant, tasty dish. I use sweet, nutty pecans to create a crispy crust for the juicy, tender chicken breasts. In addition, I use fresh goat cheese, amped up with herbs and black pepper, to serve as my "finishing" sauce by melting it atop the hot chicken right when it's cooked. Trust me, this goat cheese technique is to die for. I like to serve this dish atop a bed of roasted tomatoes and asparagus, goes right into the oven in one pan—simple, clean cooking at its finest. This meal pairs well with crisp, mineral-y white wines and light reds.

HANDS-ON 30 MIN.   TOTAL 1 HR., 45 MIN.

SERVES 4

1 Mash first 4 ingredients together in a small bowl with back of fork until mixture is blended and smooth. Spoon goat cheese mixture on bottom third of a sheet of plastic wrap. Tightly roll goat cheese mixture in plastic wrap, forming a log. Twist ends to seal. Chill 1 hour or until firm.

2 Meanwhile, place chicken breasts between 2 sheets of plastic wrap, and flatten to ¼-inch thickness, using a rolling pin or flat side of a meat mallet. Pulse pecans, breadcrumbs, and 2 tsp. salt in a food processor until finely ground; pour pecan mixture onto a large plate. Whisk together egg and 1 Tbsp. water in a bowl until blended. Place flour in a shallow dish. Dredge each chicken breast in flour, dip in egg mixture, and dredge in pecan mixture until coated, shaking off excess.

3 Snap off, and discard tough ends of asparagus. Combine asparagus, tomatoes, olives, 1 Tbsp. oil, and remaining ¼ tsp. salt; toss until coated. Spread in a single layer on a baking sheet.

4 Preheat oven to 425°. Place a cast-iron skillet over medium heat 1 minute or until hot; add 1 Tbsp. oil. Cook 2 chicken breasts in hot oil 4 minutes on each side. Transfer chicken to a baking sheet. Repeat procedure with remaining 1 Tbsp. oil and chicken breasts.

5 Bake chicken and asparagus mixture at the same time at 425°, placing chicken on bottom oven rack and asparagus mixture on top rack, for 10 minutes or until chicken is firm to the touch and desired degree of doneness. Remove chicken and asparagus mixture from oven; let chicken stand at room temperature. Stir asparagus mixture, and bake 5 more minutes or until tender.

6 Spoon asparagus mixture onto a large serving platter or individual plates. Top with cooked chicken. Unwrap chilled goat cheese, cut into ¼-inch-thick slices. Place 1 goat cheese slice on each chicken breast. Serve immediately.

⋛ INGREDIENTS ⋚

4 oz. goat cheese, softened
1 garlic clove, finely minced
1 Tbsp. finely chopped fresh thyme
1 tsp. freshly ground black pepper
4 (6-oz.) chicken breasts
1 cup chopped pecans
½ cup fine, dry breadcrumbs
2¼ tsp. kosher salt, divided
1 large egg
1 cup all-purpose flour
1 lb. fresh asparagus
1½ cups cherry tomatoes
½ cup pitted kalamata olives
3 Tbsp. extra virgin olive oil, divided

Give Thanks Fried Turkey

Sure, we catch a lot of hell down here for our affinity to drop everything into a deep fryer. But, you haven't had turkey if you haven't had it deep-fried. Nowadays, there are all sorts of schools of thought when it comes to brining and cooking the perfect bird. I'm of the opinion that deep-frying that bird solves all your problems. Peanut oil, which is healthier than say, vegetable or canola, imparts great flavor while keeping everything deliciously moist and tender. Here's my fair warning: don't try to do this indoors or inside of a garage. Just look at YouTube and see what happens to those who don't take my advice.

Use a 30-qt. propane turkey fryer, and make sure it's on steady ground. From there, I like to treat the bird quite simply when it comes to seasoning. I tested this recipe with and without traditional brine (overnight in salt, sugar, water, and spices). Unless you want to create more work for yourself or impress your guests with the fact that you've put the bird through a 36-hour cooking process, I say skip the brining step altogether. Inject the following marinade into the bird for some savory and spicy essence throughout the meat.

HANDS-ON 1 HR. TOTAL **2 HR., 20 MIN.,** PLUS **1** DAY FOR MARINATING

SERVES 10

⇝ MARINADE ⇜

2 cups unsalted butter, melted
½ cup dark amber ale
2 Tbsp. kosher salt
1 Tbsp. ground white pepper
1 Tbsp. garlic powder
1 Tbsp. onion powder
1 Tbsp. hot sauce
1 tsp. Worcestershire sauce

⇝ TURKEY ⇜

1 (12- to 13-lb.) whole fresh free-range turkey
Marinade injector
1 large oven bag
Peanut oil (about 3 to 4 gallons)

1 Prepare Marinade: Stir together melted butter and next 7 ingredients in a small bowl until blended.

2 Prepare Turkey: Remove giblets and neck from turkey, and rinse turkey with cold water. Drain cavity well; pat dry. Fill injector with Marinade, and inject turkey all over, including legs, back, wings, thighs, and breasts. Place turkey in oven bag; twist end of bag, and close with tie. Chill 24 hours.

3 Pour oil into a 30-qt. propane turkey fryer to a depth of two-thirds full. (See Gent's Tip at right.) Heat oil to 350° over a medium-low flame according to manufacturer's instructions (about 1 hour).

4 Meanwhile, remove turkey from oven bag, and pat completely dry with paper towels. Let turkey stand at room temperature 30 minutes.

5 Place turkey on fryer rod. Carefully lower turkey into hot oil with rod attachment.

6 Fry turkey 42 minutes or until a meat thermometer inserted into thickest portion of thigh registers 165° (about 3½ minutes per pound. Keep oil temperature between 300° and 325°.) Remove turkey from oil; drain.

7 Place turkey on a wire rack, and cover loosely with aluminum foil. Let stand 20 minutes before slicing.

Note: Tested with Abita Amber Ale.

Gent's Tip

To determine the proper amount of oil for cooking, place the turkey in the turkey fryer, and add water to cover completely by 1 inch—ensuring that at least 5 inches of space remain between the water line and the top of the fryer. The amount of water used to reach that point will be the exact amount of oil needed for the recipe. Drain and measure the water, remove the turkey, and ensure that the turkey is completely dry before preparing the recipe.

Roasted Quail + Pomegranate Quinoa

Consider this dish haute cuisine for hunters. One doesn't need much beyond a shotgun, a trusty dog, and an appetite for fun. I like to season my quail with a smoky dry rub, followed by a quick sear in a cast-iron skillet to finish them off until the meat is just pink, which means nice and juicy. I serve them over a bed of pomegranate seed-studded quinoa, a nutty protein-packed grain that pairs awesomely with this wild game. I spoon reserved juices and fats from the pan over the birds, which soak into the quinoa, creating a delicious sauce. Quail are best when served sharing a few fingers' of bourbon with your closest buddies after a day in the fields.

HANDS-ON 17 MIN. **TOTAL 39 MIN.**

SERVES 4

1 Preheat oven to 425°. Rinse quail with cold water, and thoroughly pat dry. Mash butter and next 6 ingredients together in a small bowl using back of a fork until blended and smooth. Rub butter mixture generously over quail. Insert an orange piece into cavity of each quail, trimming as needed to fit.

2 Place a 12-inch cast-iron skillet over medium heat 1 minute. Add quail, breast sides down, and cook 2 minutes. Turn quail breasts side up. Transfer skillet to oven and bake, uncovered, at 425° for 15 minutes or until a meat thermometer inserted into thickest portion of thigh registers 150°. (Meat will be slightly pink.) Transfer quail and pan drippings to a plate; cover loosely with aluminum foil, and let stand 10 minutes.

3 Meanwhile, bring quinoa and next 3 ingredients to a boil in a small saucepan over medium heat, stirring occasionally. Cover, reduce heat to medium-low, and simmer 20 minutes or until liquid is absorbed. Remove from heat, and fluff with a fork. Stir in pomegranate seeds, orange zest, and mint. Spoon quinoa onto a serving platter, and top with quail and pan drippings. Serve immediately.

⋛ INGREDIENTS ⋚

4 quail, dressed
4 Tbsp. unsalted butter, softened
1½ tsp. kosher salt
1 tsp. freshly ground black pepper
¼ tsp. ground cumin
½ tsp. chili powder
½ tsp. ground allspice
Pinch of ground red pepper
1 orange, quartered
1 cup uncooked quinoa
2 cups chicken stock
1 Tbsp. unsalted butter
½ tsp. kosher salt
½ cup pomegranate seeds
1 Tbsp. orange zest
1 Tbsp. finely chopped fresh mint

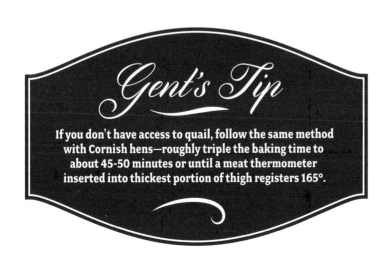

Gent's Tip

If you don't have access to quail, follow the same method with Cornish hens—roughly triple the baking time to about 45-50 minutes or until a meat thermometer inserted into thickest portion of thigh registers 165°.

Pan-Seared Duck Breasts + Southern Fried Rice

Wild duck is far and away one of my favorite delicacies. It's even better when I've hunted the duck on my own. Duck hunting is a lifestyle sport. In late fall, brave men and women, along with their trusty canine companions, battle chilly waters and frigid air to chance shooting this waterfowl. The camaraderie and abundance of delicious duck from a successful hunt is something everyone should experience.

I like to embrace an influence of Asian flavors when it comes to duck. It's all about creating that crispy, fatty crust on the duck breasts. I use a heavy-bottomed cast-iron skillet to perfectly render and sear the fatty side of the breasts. Once they are cooked, I set them aside to rest, while I prepare a quick stir-fry in the duck fat drippings. Let me tell you—it ain't gonna get any better than fried rice prepared in duck fat. For this recipe, make sure all of your ingredients are prepped prior to cooking.

HANDS-ON **36 MIN.** TOTAL **36 MIN.**

SERVES **4**

⇒ INGREDIENTS ⇐

4 (6-oz.) wild duck breasts
2 Tbsp. teriyaki sauce
2½ tsp. freshly ground black pepper, divided
1 large Vidalia or sweet onion, finely diced
2 carrots, finely diced
½ red bell pepper, finely diced
1 cup thinly sliced okra
2 garlic cloves, minced
2 Tbsp. soy sauce
⅛ tsp. dried crushed red pepper
2 cups cooked rice, at room temperature
2 large eggs, beaten

1 Make shallow cuts in fat of duck breasts with a paring knife, cutting just down to flesh. Place breasts in a shallow dish, and drizzle with teriyaki sauce; sprinkle with 2 tsp. black pepper. Toss until well coated.

2 Place a 12-inch cast-iron skillet over medium heat 2 minutes or until hot. Place breasts, fat sides down in skillet, and cook, undisturbed, 10 minutes. Turn breasts over, and cook 5 more minutes or until a meat thermometer inserted into thickest portion registers 125°. Remove skillet from heat; transfer breasts to a plate, and keep warm. Transfer drippings from skillet to a heatproof container.

3 Return skillet to heat, and increase temperature to medium-high; add 2 Tbsp. reserved drippings. Add onion, carrot, bell pepper, and okra; sauté 6 minutes or until vegetables are just tender. Add garlic, and stir in soy sauce, red pepper, and remaining ½ tsp. black pepper. Add rice, stirring until coated. Push rice mixture to sides of pan, making a well in center of mixture.

4 Add eggs to center of mixture, and cook, stirring occasionally, 1-2 minutes or until set. Stir egg into rice mixture. Remove from heat.

5 Slice breasts diagonally across the grain into ½-inch slices, reserving any juices. Spoon rice mixture onto serving plates, and top with sliced duck; drizzle with reserved drippings. Serve immediately.

Gent's Tip

You should be left with a tablespoon of reserved duck fat from cooking this dish. Do not throw it out! Better than bacon or pork renderings, duck fat adds a nice depth of flavor when used as an alternative to butter or oil as a base for soups, braises, or vegetable dishes.

Chicken + Andouille Sausage Jambalaya

Since his time in New Orleans, Jon Stinchcomb makes jambalaya every year for Christmas dinner. In my recipe, I prefer to use chicken thighs as the dark meat. Creating a one-pot meal with tons of flavor is all about staging and timing. I brown my meat to create a sear and release the drippings to season and flavor the rest of the dish.

HANDS-ON 33 MIN. TOTAL 1 HR., 18 MIN.

SERVES 8-10

⇒ INGREDIENTS ⇐

- 1½ lb. andouille sausage, cut into ½-inch pieces
- 1½ lb. skinless, boneless chicken thighs, cut into bite-size chunks
- 2 Tbsp. unsalted butter
- 1 medium onion, finely diced
- 1 medium green bell pepper, finely diced
- 3 celery ribs, finely diced
- 3 garlic cloves, minced
- 3 bay leaves
- 2½ cups uncooked converted white rice
- 1 (28-oz.) can petite diced tomatoes
- 4 cups reduced-sodium fat-free chicken broth
- Hot sauce
- Garnish: sliced green onions

1 Place a Dutch oven or large heavy saucepan over medium-high heat 1 minute or until hot. Add sausage, and cook, stirring occasionally, 5 minutes or until browned. Remove sausage with a slotted spoon, and drain on a paper towel–lined plate, reserving drippings in Dutch oven. Cook chicken in reserved drippings, stirring occasionally, 5 minutes or until browned. Transfer chicken to plate with sausage, reserving drippings in Dutch oven.

2 Add butter to reserved drippings in skillet, and cook until butter melts. Add onion, bell pepper, and celery, sauté 8-10 minutes or just until vegetables are tender. Add garlic and bay leaves; sauté 1 minute or until fragrant.

3 Stir in rice with a wooden spoon, and cook, stirring frequently, until toasted and coated with pan drippings. Add tomatoes, and cook, stirring with a wooden spoon to loosen any browned bits from bottom of Dutch oven, 1 minute.

4 Stir in chicken and sausage; add broth and desired amount of hot sauce. Bring mixture to a boil over medium-high heat. Cover, reduce heat to medium-low, and simmer 25 minutes. Remove from heat, and let stand, covered, 10 minutes. Remove bay leaves before serving.

WALKING THE WALK...

JON STINCHCOMB

"**R**ight 38 Waggle Screen on Go. Ready, break!" Those hushed words echoing out of the football huddle on a late spring afternoon meant one thing...I was about to get knocked in the dirt.

As a rite of passage, my friends and I started out on the scout team. It was our job to run the opposing team's plays to ensure the senior Parkview Panthers would be ready to crush any team that stepped into the Big Orange Jungle under the Friday night lights.

But damn, on this day, and with the Right 38 Waggle Screen on Go, I was getting ready to take on a future NFL tackle, Jon Stinchcomb. Let's just say that it didn't go well.

Not long ago, but a decade and a half later, Jon and I are enjoying lunch in Atlanta, swapping stories of how those athletic challenges shaped us into the men we've become. Jon went on to become a standout offensive lineman at our alma mater, the University of Georgia, followed by eight incredible seasons and a Super Bowl Championship with the New Orleans Saints.

When asked, Jon sights a clear divide in his career with the Saints—pre-Katrina and post. He recalls that the locker room and coaching staff almost entirely changed after the storm. That 'new' team's 2006 return to the Superdome spawned the defeat of the Atlanta Falcons, thrusting the Saints back into the national spotlight as serious championship contenders. Three years later, the Saints brought home their first league championship win against the Colts in Super Bowl XLIV.

New Orleans is the city that Jon grew to love. It's quirks, history, and sense of community fit nicely with Jon's service-oriented leadership...the food isn't bad either. After the championship, Jon was surprised by locals who came up to him at the grocery store, not to offer congratulations, but rather a thank you. You see, Jon, and the Saints, were a ray of light, of hope, for a city that was looking to rebuild.

Our conversation is not all about sports chatter. At 6'5" tall and 315 lb., Stinch enjoyed his fair share of NOLA cuisine. He revealed to me a Saints Thursday night tradition, where the linesmen and quarterbacks would dine at one of the many famous New Orleans eateries. It was this breaking of bread weekly ritual that strengthened their brotherhood on and off the field.

Nowadays, Jon pays homage to his time in New Orleans every Christmas by whipping up a batch of one of his Cajun favorites, jambalaya. In addition to raising his son and daughter with high-school sweetheart Ali, Jon now spends the majority of his time devoted to charitable causes that support leadership, character development, and change for youth.

A man of service, family, faith, and one hell of a gridiron champion. I say, "Jon, thank you."

THE GAUNTLET — JONES BRIDGE PARK

In high school, I spent most weekends with my buddies at Jones Bridge Park to slay trout on the Chattahoochee River. Trout are plentiful, as the Buford Dam upriver supplies a steady dose of cold water perfect for feeding and breeding. As teenagers, we spent hours on the river, testing each other by swimming the "gauntlet" and jumping off the old Jones Bridge—an activity forbidden by my parents. We'd throw our weight around with fly rods and rooster tails, trying to catch as many fish as we could. One day, my buddy Seth Marler and I caught more than 20 trout and Seth actually caught a trout with his bare hands—no kidding. Memories like this come to mind whenever I prepare whole trout.

Baked Trout + Prosciutto + White Cheddar Grits

Most often the best way to prepare trout is to simply grill them with a bit of olive oil, salt, pepper, and lemon. But every once in a while, I dress up my trout with a few "adult" ingredients like prosciutto and green olives. By the way, these trout taste best when you catch them with your own hands!

HANDS-ON **28 MIN.** TOTAL **38 MIN.**

SERVES **2-4**

1 Preheat grill to 300°-350° (medium). Sprinkle trout inside and out with of salt and pepper. Stuff 4 lemon slices and 1 Tbsp. butter into each fish cavity. Place 4 prosciutto slices lengthwise on a large cutting board, slightly overlapping slices. Place 1 trout horizontally across prosciutto slices about one-third from bottom edge; tightly wrap prosciutto around trout, leaving head and tail unwrapped. Repeat wrapping procedure with remaining prosciutto and trout.

2 Melt remaining 2 Tbsp. butter, and brush melted butter over wrapped trout. Grill trout, covered with grill lid, 8 minutes on each side or until prosciutto is crisp and fish flakes easily with a fork.

3 Spoon White Cheddar Grits onto serving plates; top with trout. Arrange olives around trout, and serve immediately.

⇒ INGREDIENTS ⇐

2 (¾- to 1-lb.) dressed whole trout
1 tsp. kosher salt
½ tsp. freshly ground black pepper
1 lemon, cut crosswise into 8 thin slices
4 Tbsp. unsalted butter, divided
8 thin prosciutto slices (about 4 oz.)
White Cheddar Grits
12 large, pitted Spanish olives

White Cheddar Grits

HANDS-ON **10 MIN.** TOTAL **10 MIN.**

MAKES **4 CUPS**

1 Bring 3 cups water to a rolling boil over high heat. Gradually whisk in grits. Reduce heat to medium-low, and cook, stirring frequently, 5 minutes or until creamy and tender.

2 Add butter, salt, and cheese, stirring until blended and butter and cheese melt. Serve immediately.

⇒ INGREDIENTS ⇐

1 cup uncooked quick-cooking grits
1½ Tbsp. unsalted butter
1 tsp. kosher salt
1 cup (4 oz.) shredded sharp white
   Cheddar cheese
Garnish: freshly ground black pepper

Crispy Speckled Trout + Tartar Sauce

There's no better way to kill an afternoon than on a boat in the flats of Louisiana wrangling in "spec" after "spec," the sportsman's nickname for this specics, while staying hydrated with a cooler full of cold Army pops, aka cold beers. Fortunately specs are abundant throughout the state, allowing the daily catch limits per person to reach a level that calls out for a large fish fry later in the evening. That being said, I must preach conservation. Be a responsible sportsman, and gentleman, for that matter, always carry a license, and ensure that your limits and catch sizes are in line with the state's rules and regulations.

After cleaning and filleting these little guys on the dock, I go with a simple beer-mustard wet wash, followed by a dip in a crispy cornmeal batter prior to hitting the hot oil. I pair up the crispy fried fish with my deliciously creamy tartar sauce. Great fun and great food shared with even better friends—that's my idea of happiness.

HANDS-ON 30 MIN. TOTAL **35 MIN.**

SERVES 10

⋛ INGREDIENTS ⋚

5 lb. speckled trout fillets
1 cup Creole mustard*
½ cup amber beer
¼ cup fresh lemon juice
2 cups plain yellow cornmeal
1 cup all-purpose flour
2 Tbsp. Creole seasoning
1 tsp. ground red pepper
Peanut oil
Tartar Sauce

*Yellow mustard may be substituted.

1 Preheat oven to 200°. Combine first 4 ingredients in a large bowl, and mix well. Stir together cornmeal and next 3 ingredients in a shallow dish until blended.

2 Place a 12-inch cast-iron skillet over medium heat; add oil to depth of 2 inches. Heat oil to 350°.

3 Remove fish from mustard mixture, allowing excess to drip off; dredge in cornmeal mixture, shaking off excess.

4 Fry fish, in batches of 3 or 4, for 2 minutes on each side or until golden brown. Transfer to a wire rack in a jelly-roll pan, and keep warm in a 200° oven. Serve with Tartar Sauce.

Note: Tested with Abita Amber Beer.

Tartar Sauce

HANDS-ON 5 MIN. TOTAL **5 MIN.**

MAKES 1 CUP

⋛ INGREDIENTS ⋚

1 cup mayonnaise
¼ cup finely chopped dill pickles
2 Tbsp. grated Vidalia or sweet onion
3 Tbsp. fresh lemon juice
1 tsp. hot sauce

1 Stir together all ingredients in a small bowl. Cover and chill until ready to serve.

Blackened Catfish + Salsa Fresca

Back in the 1980s, New Orleans chef Paul Prudhomme invented a blackening method that involved slathering freshly caught redfish with melted butter and coating them liberally with spices. Next, he cooked the fish in a cast-iron pan that was literally screeching hot—so hot Prudhomme suggested seeing a bit of white ash around the edge of the pan when it was preheating. Such a method defies all logic—using low smoke point butter and a heavy seasoning blend over extreme heat to cook a delicate piece of fish? Yet, the result is surprisingly fantastic, resulting in a "blackening craze" seen on menus everywhere.

Blackening is one of my favorite ways to enjoy a piece of fish. Rather than take the chance of having a visit from my fire department or an angry neighbor, I like to make this dish on my grill. I put my favorite piece of cast-iron cookware right on the grill. Instead of the traditional Cajun rub, I like to use my own spice blend and Salsa Fresca, which provides a light, cool element.

HANDS-ON **22 MIN.**   TOTAL **22 MIN.**

SERVES **4**

1 Prepare Salsa Fresca: Stir together tomatoes and next 6 ingredients in a serving bowl. Cover and let stand at room temperature until ready to serve.

2 Prepare Blackened Catfish: Preheat grill to 400°-450° (high). Place a 12-inch cast-iron skillet on grate of grill. Cover with grill lid, and heat skillet 5-7 minutes or until skillet begins to smoke.

3 Meanwhile, stir together pepper and next 4 ingredients in a large dish. Dip fish in melted butter, and dredge in pepper mixture, shaking off excess.

4 Add 2 fish to skillet, and cook 2 minutes on each side or until fish flakes easily with a fork. (Fish will sizzle and smoke.) Transfer fish to a serving platter, and keep warm. Repeat procedure with remaining fish. Serve fish topped with Salsa Fresca.

⋛ SALSA FRESCA ⋚

4 plum tomatoes, finely chopped
2 Tbsp. finely diced red onion
3 garlic cloves, minced
½ jalapeño pepper, seeded and minced
2 Tbsp. finely chopped fresh cilantro
2 Tbsp. fresh lime juice
½ tsp. kosher salt

⋛ BLACKENED CATFISH ⋚

2 tsp. freshly ground black pepper
2 tsp. kosher salt
¼ cup chili powder
2 Tbsp. ground cumin
2 Tbsp. dried Mexican oregano
4 (6-oz.) catfish fillets
½ cup butter, melted

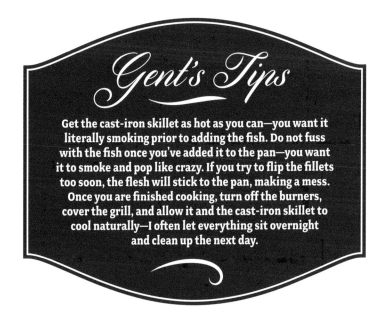

Gent's Tips

Get the cast-iron skillet as hot as you can—you want it literally smoking prior to adding the fish. Do not fuss with the fish once you've added it to the pan—you want it to smoke and pop like crazy. If you try to flip the fillets too soon, the flesh will stick to the pan, making a mess. Once you are finished cooking, turn off the burners, cover the grill, and allow it and the cast-iron skillet to cool naturally—I often let everything sit overnight and clean up the next day.

Creole Redfish + Crab Salad

Although I'm always partial to a good fish fry, I also realize that dunking chunks of freshly caught redfish in peanut oil isn't ideal for my waistline. Instead, I simply pan-sear it, which imparts just a bit of savory flavor to the mild, tender fish. I like to top the fish with a chilled crab salad to create a nice temperature contrast, impressive presentation, and, of course, big flavor. For those of you who don't have redfish on hand, try a flaky white fish such as tilapia, flounder, or sea bass. This dish pairs well with crisp white and rosé wines or bold pilsner or lager beers.

HANDS-ON 13 MIN. TOTAL 21 MIN.

SERVES 4

CRAB SALAD

1 lb. fresh jumbo lump crabmeat
½ cup finely diced celery
½ cup finely diced red bell pepper
½ cup finely diced red onion
1 tsp. kosher salt
½ tsp. freshly ground black pepper
1 Tbsp. fresh lemon juice
¼ cup mayonnaise

REDFISH

¼ cup unsalted butter
4 (8-oz.) redfish fillets
1 tsp. Creole seasoning
1 Tbsp. finely chopped fresh parsley

1 Prepare Crab Salad: Pick crabmeat, removing any bits of shell. Stir together crab and next 7 ingredients in a large bowl until blended, being careful not to break apart crab. Cover and chill until ready to serve. Salad can be prepared up to 1 day in advance; refrigerate in an airtight container.

2 Prepare Redfish: Melt butter in a large skillet over medium-high heat. Sprinkle both sides of fish fillets with Creole seasoning. Cook fish in hot skillet 3-4 minutes on each side or until browned and fish flakes easily with a fork. Sprinkle with parsley.

3 Place fish fillets on individual plates, and top each with chilled crab salad. Serve immediately.

THE LOUISIANA REDFISH

I'm probably at my happiest when out on a skiff surrounded by cold beers and friends, reeling in a big ole redfish for dinner. Reds are always known for being great fighters, making them a favorite catch for sport fishermen. And one doesn't have to travel very far outside my favorite city, New Orleans, to find some of the country's best red fishing. Within the small town of Delacroix in Saint Bernard

Parish, you'll find Captain Jack and his team at Sweetwater Marina. Jack will not only put you onto some big reds, but he's also likely to bust your chops throughout the day—he nicknamed me "pretty boy," not as bad as the other guy in the boat who got "booger." Regardless, Jack knows his stuff, which always leaves us with plenty of fish to yield in this delicious recipe.

GEECHIE BOY MARKET & MILL

Much like New Orleans gumbo, shrimp and grits takes on many a variation throughout South Carolina and beyond. For some of the best grits in the South, I call out Geechie Boy Market and Mill grits (see page 278). Husband-and-wife Greg and Betsy Johnsman use a 60-plus-year-old mill on their family farm on Edisto Island to turn out grits the old-fashioned way. Of course, if you don't have access to their superb milled goods, which are sold at their market and online, any stone-ground grits will do—especially when you add in a bit of love, as I do here.

Lowcountry Shrimp + Geechie Boy Grits

My recipe is a summation of all the shrimp and grits dishes I've enjoyed throughout the Lowcountry. Served any time of the day, this meal perfectly embodies working with what the good Lord provides. Dish it up with a Bloody Mary or Mimosa in the morning, or fancy it up with a glass of crisp Sauvignon Blanc or Chardonnay in the afternoon or evening.

HANDS-ON 25 MIN. **TOTAL 55 MIN.**

SERVES 4

1 Melt 2 Tbsp. butter in a medium-size saucepan over medium heat. Stir in grits, and cook, stirring constantly, 1-2 minutes or until toasted. Whisk in 3 cups water, making sure no lumps form. Bring mixture to a light boil, and stir in salt and pepper. Reduce heat to medium-low, and simmer, stirring often, 30 minutes or until grits are tender and creamy. Stir in cream, and blend well.

2 Meanwhile, peel shrimp, leaving tails on; devein, if desired. Place a 12-inch cast-iron skillet over medium heat 1 minute or until hot. Add bacon, and cook, stirring often and turning pieces as needed, 5 minutes or until crisp. Remove bacon with a slotted spoon, and drain on paper towels, reserving drippings in skillet.

3 Sauté shrimp in reserved drippings 2 minutes or just until shrimp turn pink. Transfer shrimp to a plate, reserving drippings in skillet.

4 Add remaining 2 Tbsp. butter to reserved drippings in skillet, and cook until butter melts. Whisk in flour, and cook, whisking constantly, 6 minutes or until flour is caramel colored. Add onion and bell pepper, and sauté 6 minutes or until tender. Add garlic, tomatoes, and seasoning; sauté 5 minutes or until tomatoes are slightly softened.

5 Add wine, and cook, stirring with a wooden spoon to loosen any browned bits from bottom of skillet, 1 minute. Gradually stir in stock, and bring mixture to a light boil. Stir in shrimp, reduce heat to low, and simmer 3 minutes or until shrimp turn bright pink and opaque.

6 Spoon grits into shallow bowls, and top with shrimp mixture; sprinkle with bacon. Serve immediately.

⇒ INGREDIENTS ⇐

4 Tbsp. unsalted butter, divided
1 cup uncooked stone-ground grits
1½ tsp. kosher salt
½ tsp. freshly ground black pepper
1 cup heavy cream
1 lb. unpeeled extra-large raw shrimp
4 hickory-smoked bacon slices, chopped
2 Tbsp. all-purpose flour
1 medium Vidalia or sweet onion, finely diced
½ green bell pepper, finely diced
2 garlic cloves, minced
1½ cups seeded, diced fresh tomatoes
½ tsp. Creole seasoning
½ cup dry white wine
1 cup Quick Shrimp Stock (page 79)*
Garnish: finely chopped green onions

*Reduced-sodium chicken broth may be substituted.

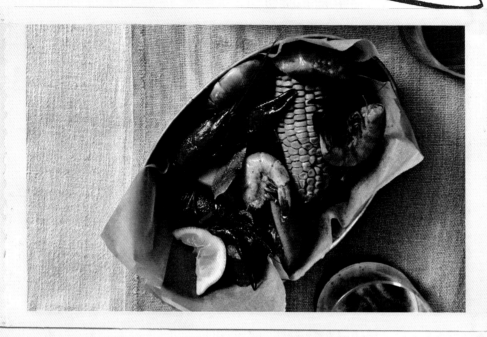

I can think of nothing better than sharing good food and cold beer with 10 or 200 of my best friends. I love this recipe because the eating experience is communal, and cleanup is quick and easy—just roll up the newspaper with all the leftovers on the table, and toss it in the trash can.

In college, this was my go-to meal when it came to entertaining. My band would travel the Southeast, playing college towns and making friends at the many local clubs, restaurants, and bars. Whenever we found ourselves near the Gulf Coast, we'd stop off at the local fishing docks and pick up a mess of fresh seafood—let's just say those 12-passenger van rides back to Athens smelled like the ocean, amongst other things! While en route, we'd text and call our friends to arrange a big keg party upon arrival.

Most recently, I've taken this recipe up to the shores of Prince Edward Island in Canada and cooked it with local seafood and potatoes for thousands of festivalgoers at the Cavendish Beach Music Festival, Canada's largest country music event. Yes, it takes a Nashville guy to cook up local Canadian seafood for the likes of Alabama, Dierks Bentley, Brad Paisley, and other acts!

Lowcountry Boil

I will forever be indebted to the kind folks who have shared their opinions, philosophies, and methods about making the perfect boil. I can say that mine is a mix of Louisiana (the crawfish and sausage blend) and the Lowcountry styles (Georgia and South Carolina). Such a mixture is the sum of my experiences, travels, tastes, and preferences. That reminds me—boils are always remembered by number and season, and this is the third boil of the season.

HANDS-ON 25 MIN. TOTAL 1 HR.
SERVES 20

1 Add water to a 44-qt. stockpot, filling almost two-thirds full. Add salt and next 8 ingredients; cover and bring to a rolling boil over high heat (about 25 minutes).

2 Add potatoes and onions; return to a boil, and cook 8 minutes. Add corn and sausage; return to a boil, and cook 5 minutes.

3 Add crawfish; return to a boil, and cook 3 minutes. Add shrimp, turn off heat, and cover. Let stand, covered and undisturbed, 10-30 minutes. (The longer it stands, the more flavorful the boil will be.)

4 Uncover and stir mixture to be sure all crawfish are bright red and shrimp are pink and firm.

5 Spread newspaper on a large table, and arrange lemon wedges around edge of table. Sprinkle desired amount of Cajun seasoning over newspaper inside ring of lemon wedges. Drain mixture, and pour onto newspaper-lined table; remove and discard bay leaves. Sprinkle mixture with desired amount of Cajun seasoning. Eat—and drink—up!

Note: To purge crawfish of mud and debris, place them in a 48-qt. cooler with a pourable spout. Add cold water and 2 cups salt. Gently stir crawfish; let stand 3 minutes. Open spout, tilt cooler, and rinse crawfish with a steady stream of cold water until water runs clear.

⇒ INGREDIENTS ⇐

- 1½ cups kosher salt
- 10 bay leaves
- 2 garlic bulbs
- 1 bunch celery
- 6 lemons, cut in half
- ½ cup black peppercorns
- 1 cup smoked paprika
- ½ cup ground red pepper
- 6 (12-oz.) cans or bottles light beer
- 5 lb. small red potatoes
- 5 lb. Vidalia or sweet onions, quartered
- 5 lb. fresh corn, husks removed and halved
- 5 lb. andouille or smoked sausage, cut into 2-inch pieces
- 10 lb. live fresh crawfish, purged
- 5 lb. unpeeled, large raw Gulf shrimp with heads and tails
- Newspaper
- Fresh lemon wedges
- Cajun seasoning

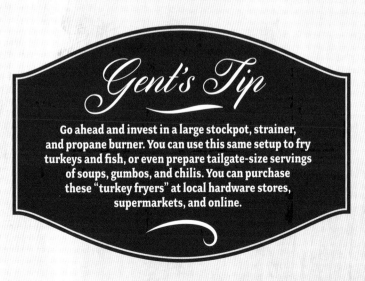

Gent's Tip

Go ahead and invest in a large stockpot, strainer, and propane burner. You can use this same setup to fry turkeys and fish, or even prepare tailgate-size servings of soups, gumbos, and chilis. You can purchase these "turkey fryers" at local hardware stores, supermarkets, and online.

Quick Cook Shrimp + Chorizo Paella

Brimming with fresh seafood, paella is a real crowd-pleaser, often served to hundreds of people during festivals and important holidays. I like to build on great Spanish flavors with local Southern ingredients like Gulf shrimp, Vidalia onion, and green peas. I also substitute some store-bought ones like yellow rice mix, which speeds up the whole process, making paella a weeknight-friendly meal. Rest assured, taking a few shortcuts here and there won't sacrifice any flavor. Pair this dish with amber ale or Rioja wine.

HANDS-ON 42 MIN. TOTAL **42 MIN.**

SERVES 6

1 Peel shrimp, leaving tails on; devein, if desired.

2 Place a large skillet over medium-high heat 1-2 minutes or until hot. Add chorizo, and cook, stirring constantly, 3 minutes or until browned. Transfer chorizo to a paper towel–lined plate, reserving drippings in skillet.

3 Add onion to reserved hot drippings in skillet, and sauté 5 minutes or until translucent and tender. Stir in rice mix, and cook, stirring constantly, 1-2 minutes or until rice is well coated.

4 Add tomatoes, and cook, stirring with a wooden spoon to loosen any browned bits from bottom of skillet, 1 minute. Add chicken broth, and bring to a boil over high heat. Cover, reduce heat to low, and simmer, stirring once, 15 minutes.

5 Fold chorizo, shrimp, and peas into rice mixture; cover and cook 5 minutes or until rice is al dente and shrimp turn bright pink and firm. Serve immediately.

INGREDIENTS

1 lb. unpeeled, large raw Gulf shrimp
½ lb. dried chorizo sausage, cut into ½-inch slices
1 medium Vidalia or sweet onion, finely diced
1 (5-oz.) package yellow rice mix
1 (14.5-oz.) can petite diced tomatoes, undrained
2¼ cups reduced-sodium chicken broth
1½ cups fresh or frozen green peas
Garnish: chopped fresh parsley

Great-Grandma Addie's Salmon Croquettes

Once an affordable yet hearty dish, salmon croquettes have seen many an "artisanal" makeover these days using fresh-cooked organic salmon along with ingredients that may or may not be indigenous to the region. The way I see it, why mess with a good thing? I like to keep my recipe straightforward and simple, presenting a dish in the same manner that satisfied me and the many generations that came before me.

HANDS-ON 21 MIN. TOTAL **26 MIN.**

SERVES **4**

⇒ INGREDIENTS ⇐

- 3 (5-oz.) aluminum foil pouches skinless, boneless pink salmon
- ½ cup fine, dry breadcrumbs
- 1 large egg, beaten
- 1 tsp. kosher salt
- ½ tsp. freshly ground black pepper
- 2 Tbsp. finely chopped green bell pepper
- 2 Tbsp. finely chopped red bell pepper
- ½ medium Vidalia or sweet onion, finely grated
- 1 Tbsp. fresh lemon juice
- ¼ cup unsalted butter, divided
- Creamy Dill and Lemon Sauce

1 Place salmon in a wire-mesh strainer, and press lightly to remove excess liquid. Combine salmon and next 8 ingredients in a large bowl. Using hands, toss ingredients together until blended, being careful not to overwork mixture. Loosely shape mixture into 8 (3-inch) patties each about 1-inch thick.

2 Place a 10-inch cast-iron skillet over medium heat 1 minute or until hot; melt 2 Tbsp. butter in hot skillet. Add half of salmon patties, and cook 4 minutes on each side or until browned. Transfer patties to a serving platter, and cover loosely with aluminum foil to keep warm. Repeat procedure with remaining butter and patties.

3 Serve croquettes with Creamy Dill and Lemon Sauce.

Creamy Dill + Lemon Sauce

HANDS-ON 5 MIN. TOTAL **5 MIN.**

MAKES **1 CUP**

⇒ INGREDIENTS ⇐

- ¾ cup mayonnaise
- 2 Tbsp. fresh lemon juice
- 2 Tbsp. finely chopped fresh dill weed
- ¼ tsp. freshly ground black pepper

1 Stir together all ingredients in a small bowl until blended. Cover and chill until ready to serve.

Note: We tested with Duke's Mayonnaise.

Country Comfort

My great grandparents, Ira and Addie Moore

Fresh salmon was hard to find in the South until the advent of supermarkets. Most folks were introduced to this fish by way of canned pink salmon, as an alternative to canned tuna.

My grandfather still reminisces about the salmon croquettes his mother, Addie, served. This dish was a welcome reprieve from chicken, beef, or Mississippi fried catfish. Although Addie is no longer around, I was able to replicate the dish to meet Papa's exacting standards.

LUKE BRYAN

It's a muggy May evening at the LSU stadium in Baton Rouge, Louisiana. I'm standing on the tour bus with superstar Luke Bryan, surrounded by his band, minutes before he runs out to perform in front of a crowd of 55,000 fans. Just a few hours earlier, Luke and I were frying up catfish and hushpuppies to a golden perfection.

I first met Luke a decade ago when my buddy Henry Glascock, a music agent, asked me to open a show at the Georgia Theatre. Back in those days, there were no record deals, no tour buses, and no 'on-site' catering! Yet, I always knew that Luke was a solid guy who would one day make his mark on country music. Luke was kind enough to invite me to open many-a-show.

But that's how it goes with Luke Bryan—everybody is family. Currently, Luke sits atop the country charts, but his biggest priority as a Southern gentleman is his own family. Caroline, his wife and college sweetheart, and his boys Bo and Tate are all that matter when the lights go down and the sounds from the crowd finally cease. Dedication to family was taught at an early age—the son of a peanut farmer from Albany, GA—Luke grew up on the values of hard work while showcasing generosity to others. And though his songs are often upbeat, Luke is no stranger to pain—having tragically lost his only two siblings.

As an artist, Luke channels all of his life experience into his music. In a two-hour performance, Luke encourages his fans to not take themselves too seriously, to have fun, and forget about their troubles.

Nowadays, Luke has much more talented musicians opening his shows, and every now and then, I'll get a call from him (he refers to me as "Chef") when he is looking for a recipe. Of course, I'm honored and happy to oblige. Cheers to the Country Man!

Friday Fish Fry + Hush-Us-Up Hushpuppies

Friday fish fries are a common practice throughout the South, due mainly in part to Catholic tradition. This 'event' brings folks together to share in the crispy, tender deliciousness of freshly fried fish. Always better when caught and fileted by your own hands, there's also plenty of great farm-raised catfish that's raised in the great state of Mississippi. When I can't catch my own, I buy from Southern fisheries. Like most of my recipes, I like to add a little spice and heat to my fried catfish with my own special seasoning blend. I can't believe I'm giving away my secret recipe! Anyways, follow my instructions, invite over your friends, and put on a soundtrack of Luke Bryan.

HANDS-ON 15 MIN. **TOTAL 1 HR.**

SERVES 20

1 Preheat oven to 275°. Place a wire rack-lined baking sheet into oven. Place a 12-inch cast-iron skillet over medium heat; add oil to depth of 2 inches. Heat oil to 350°.

2 Combine next 6 ingredients in a large shallow bowl and mix well. Cut fish fillets into 2-inch strips. Dredge fillets in flour mixture until completely covered, shaking off excess. Carefully place the strips into hot oil; do not overcrowd. Fry fish, in batches, 2-3 minutes on each side, or until they float and are golden brown. Transfer to wire rack-lined baking sheet, and keep warm in a 275° oven. Reserve oil for frying hushpuppies. Prior to serving, season fillets to taste with Creole blend seasoning.

3 For hushpuppies, combine all ingredients in a large mixing bowl. Using a tablespoon, scoop mixture into small balls and drop batter into hot oil; do not overcrowd. Fry the hushpuppies, in batches, turning occasionally, for 2-3 minutes, or until golden brown. Serve with fried fish.

⇒ FRIED FISH ⇐

Peanut oil, for frying
2 cups yellow cornmeal
½ cup all-purpose flour
1 Tbsp. kosher salt
1 tsp. garlic powder
1 tsp. cayenne pepper
1 tsp. smoked paprika
8 fresh catfish fillets, rinsed under cold
   running water
Creole blend seasoning

⇒ HUSHPUPPIES ⇐

¾ cup yellow cornmeal
¾ cup all-purpose flour
1½ tsp. kosher salt
1½ tsp. baking powder
1 Tbsp. sugar
2 Tbsp. finely chopped green onions
1 large egg
¾ cup light beer

Pan-Seared Pork Chops + Risotto + Sautéed Spinach

This meal always reminds me of a traditional Southern New Year's Day supper, without the pounding hangover from the night before. Pork, greens, and black-eyed peas symbolize a bright future, wealth, and good luck in Southern culture. I figure most of us can use that type of good fortune throughout the year, so this meal is the perfect way to combine such tradition and charm in a delicious all-in-one package.

If you've never made risotto, you're in for a real treat. The key is patience. Stand by the stove, stirring constantly, while the rice slowly cooks. This will guarantee a dish with a creamy, rich texture.

HANDS-ON **1 HR.** TOTAL **1 HR.**

SERVES **4**

⇒ RISOTTO ⇐

8 cups chicken stock
2 Tbsp. extra virgin olive oil
1 medium Vidalia or sweet onion, finely diced
2 garlic cloves, minced
¾ tsp. kosher salt
½ tsp. freshly ground black pepper
2 cups uncooked Arborio rice
¾ cup Sauvignon Blanc wine
1 (15-oz.) can black-eyed peas, drained and rinsed

⇒ PORK CHOPS ⇐

2 Tbsp. extra virgin olive oil
1 Tbsp. balsamic vinegar
4 (6-oz.) boneless pork chops
1½ tsp. kosher salt
1 tsp. freshly ground black pepper

⇒ SAUTÉED SPINACH ⇐

1 Tbsp. extra virgin olive oil
1 garlic clove, minced
2 (6-oz.) packages fresh baby spinach
Pinch of kosher salt
1 Tbsp. fresh lemon juice

1 Prepare Risotto: Bring stock to a simmer in a large saucepan over medium-high heat. Reduce heat to low; gently simmer until ready to use. Place a large skillet over medium-high heat 2 minutes or until hot; add 2 Tbsp. oil. Add onion, and sauté 5 minutes or until tender and translucent. Add garlic, and sprinkle with ¾ tsp. salt and ½ tsp. pepper. Add rice, and cook, stirring constantly, 2-3 minutes or until rice begins to look opaque. Add wine, and cook, stirring with a wooden spoon to loosen any browned bits from bottom of skillet, 1 minute. Bring to a simmer over medium-high heat, and cook, stirring frequently, 2 minutes or until liquid is reduced by half. Add 1 cup hot stock, and return to a simmer; reduce heat to medium, and cook, stirring constantly, until liquid is absorbed. Repeat procedure, adding enough of remaining stock 1 cup at a time, until liquid is absorbed and rice is al dente and creamy (all of the stock may not be used). Total cooking time is 30-35 minutes. Stir in black-eyed peas. Keep risotto warm.

2 Prepare Pork Chops: Place a 12-inch cast-iron skillet over medium-high heat 2 minutes or until hot. Whisk together 2 Tbsp. oil and vinegar in a large shallow dish; add pork chops, and toss in oil mixture. Sprinkle both sides of chops with 1½ tsp. salt and 1 tsp. pepper. Cook chops in hot skillet 4 minutes on each side or until a meat thermometer inserted into thickest portion registers 145°. Transfer chops to a plate, reserving drippings in skillet. Cover chops loosely with aluminum foil, and let stand 5 minutes.

3 Meanwhile, prepare Sautéed Spinach: Add 1 Tbsp. oil to reserved drippings in skillet, and cook over medium-high heat until hot. Add garlic, and sauté 45 seconds, being careful not to burn garlic. Add spinach, and sauté 3 minutes or just until tender. Sprinkle with pinch of salt and 1 Tbsp. lemon juice. Remove from heat.

4 Spoon risotto into 4 shallow bowls, divide spinach among bowls, and top each with a pork chop. Serve immediately.

Bone-In Pork Chops + Sweet Heat Peaches

Savory and sweet with just a bit of heat—that's my idea of the perfect culinary trifecta. Pork, peaches, and jalapeño pepper star in this perfectly balanced trio.

When summer rolls around, I'm always on the hunt for fresh peaches. In my experience, pork and peaches share a nice affinity. For that reason, I like cooking the chops and peaches in a cast-iron skillet to create a one-pan dish that is sure to satisfy all of your senses in each bite. Heck, I even serve the skillet tableside, inviting my guests to dig right in.

Cooking the chops with the bone in adds great flavor, while ensuring the meat turns out juicy and tender. The thinly sliced fresh jalapeño adds just the right amount of heat and also provides the perfect pop of color that makes for a great presentation. This dish pairs well with cold porter beer or spicy Malbec wine.

HANDS-ON **10 MIN.** TOTAL **30 MIN.**

SERVES **4**

1 Combine first 5 ingredients in a small bowl until blended. Liberally sprinkle both sides of pork chops with brown sugar mixture.

2 Place a 12-inch cast-iron skillet over medium heat 1 minute or until hot; melt 1 Tbsp. butter in hot skillet. Add peaches to skillet, and cook, without stirring, 5 minutes or until peaches are lightly browned and caramelized. Transfer peaches to a plate.

3 Increase heat to medium-high, and melt remaining 1 Tbsp. butter in skillet. Add chops to skillet, and cook, undisturbed, 4 minutes. Reduce heat to medium, turn chops over, and return peaches to skillet. Cook 5 more minutes or a meat thermometer inserted into thickest portion of chops registers 145°.

4 Remove skillet from heat, and sprinkle with thinly sliced jalapeño pepper. Serve immediately.

⇒ INGREDIENTS ⇐

1 Tbsp. light brown sugar

1½ tsp. kosher salt

1 tsp. chili powder

½ tsp. ground cumin

½ tsp. freshly ground black pepper

4 (8-oz.) bone-in center-cut pork chops (about 1-inch thick)

2 Tbsp. unsalted butter, divided

2 ripe peaches, peeled and coarsely chopped (2 cups)

½ fresh jalapeño pepper, very thinly sliced

Slow-Roasted Pork Shoulder + Peach Salsa

Good things come to those who wait, which y'all will learn the minute you take a bite of this fall-off-the-bone tender pork. Though traditionally prepared on a smoker, I'm smart enough to realize that not all of us have such means to prepare this favorite. So instead, I pop it in the oven in the morning so I'm eating like a hog in heaven come suppertime and meals beyond.

I like pairing this with my fresh peach salsa—it's chunky and has a kick of heat and acidic bite, both of which play nicely with the juicy pork. This dish is perfectly suited to eat as-is or served between a couple of slices of Texas Toast. Whole-grain bread or a bun work, too.

HANDS-ON 20 MIN. **TOTAL 6 HR., 40 MIN.**
SERVES 8-10

INGREDIENTS

1 (9.75-lb.) bone-in pork shoulder roast (Boston butt)
6 garlic cloves, cut in half lengthwise
2 Tbsp. kosher salt
1 Tbsp. freshly ground black pepper
¼ cup extra virgin olive oil
Peach Salsa

1 Preheat oven to 325°. Using a paring knife, cut 12 (3-inch-deep) slits all over roast; insert 1 garlic half in each slit. Sprinkle roast with salt and pepper. Place an oven-safe Dutch oven over medium heat 2 minutes or until hot; add oil. Cook roast in hot oil 2-3 minutes on 3 sides or until browned (do not brown fat cap side of roast). Position roast, fat cap side up, and cover with lid.

2 Transfer to oven. Bake, covered, at 325° for 5½ hours. Transfer roast to a cutting board, and let stand until cool enough to handle (about 30 minutes). Shred roast with 2 forks, removing any large pieces of fat. Serve shredded roast with Peach Salsa.

Peach Salsa

HANDS-ON 10 MIN. **TOTAL 20 MIN.**
MAKES 2½ CUPS

INGREDIENTS

3 cups peeled and diced fresh, ripe peaches (about 6 peaches)
½ jalapeño pepper, finely minced
1 garlic clove, minced
¼ cup finely diced red onion
Pinch of kosher salt
2 Tbsp. fresh lime juice (1 lime)
1 tsp. red wine vinegar

1 Stir together all ingredients in a large bowl. Let stand at room temperature 10 minutes to allow flavors to meld. Serve salsa immediately, or cover and chill up to 5 hours.

WALKING THE WALK...

ERNEST PILLOW

If you want the most delicious, fall-off-the-bone smoked meats (and sauce), served with a side of one-liners and a ride to any destination in Nashville—call this number: 615.578.1181. Within minutes, you'll meet my buddy, Ernest Pillow.

During my bachelor days, Ernest became my tried-and-true friend to call when I needed a cab home. A few rides were all it took for us to become friends.

Ernest is one of those proud and few folks in the South who can only be appropriately classified as "a character." Trust me; such a distinction is a high honor down here, one Ernest earned over time, and one that came with honesty and good humor.

For Ernest, food is the great equalizer. I learned this after he offered me a plate of the most delicious BBQ I'd ever eaten—this because I'd asked time and time again why his cab smelled "heavenly." It turned out that Ernest had plates of BBQ, greens, sauce, etc. in the back of his ride! It don't get no better than eating pulled pork while staring at the

blurred lights of Lower Broadway! As it is, I tried it once—and as he says, "Once they try it...they gonna buy it!"

Sitting in Ernest's backyard on an early spring afternoon, just blocks away from my home, Ernest and I are jabbing at each other, as we always do, about cooking and fishing, just as much as we are respecting each other. Ernest, a man who beat alcohol addiction, has come to find peace and harmony by sharing his food with others.

Our connection through food might have sparked our friendship, yet over the years I've also learned that Ernest's respect for others is one of his most admirable qualities. He's kind enough to let others "be"—but never afraid to share his passion and love for those who might be suffering or indifferent. Ernest spends his time mentoring young African Americans at the Church of God in Nashville. I've come to realize that Ernest has the secret to life all figured out: Be kinder than necessary, without judgment or prejudice, project positivity, and always be willing to invite a stranger to the table.

Try it...and I promise y'all will buy it.

Ernest's Baby Back Ribs

Ernest Pillow has been perfecting his secret recipe since the 1970s. I was able to get enough information out of him, while reverse engineering my own concoction after tasting his delicious ribs, to come up with this recipe.

HANDS-ON 16 MIN.   TOTAL 14 HR., 41 MIN.

SERVES 8

1 Prepare Rub: Combine salt and next 6 ingredients in a small bowl, stirring with a fork to break apart and blending thoroughly.

2 Prepare Ribs: Remove thin membrane from back of ribs by slicing into it with a paring knife, and then pulling it off. (This will make ribs more tender and allow the smoke to penetrate the meat.) Rub both sides of ribs with oil; Sprinkle both sides of ribs liberally with rub mixture, and rub into ribs. Place ribs on a baking sheet, cover with aluminum foil, and chill 8-24 hours. Soak hickory chips in water 30 minutes. Light 1 side of grill, heating to 250° (low), leaving other side unlit; keep inside grill temperature between 225° and 250°. Drain hickory chips, and place in center of a 14-inch piece of heavy-duty foil; wrap tightly to form a packet. Pierce several holes in top of packet; place directly on lit side of grill.

3 Meanwhile, let ribs stand at room temperature 30 minutes. Place ribs, bone sides down, over unlit side of grill, overlapping slabs slightly if needed. Grill ribs, covered with grill lid, 5 hours or until ribs bend slightly in middle when lifted with tongs from 1 end; ribs will be deep brown in color and crisp on edges. (If ribs do not bend, continue to grill, covered with grill lid, checking every 20 minutes.) Remove ribs from grill, and cover loosely with foil; let stand 10 minutes. To serve, cut each slab into thirds, slicing between bones. Serve with warm Habanero Barbecue Sauce.

RUB

2 Tbsp. kosher salt
2 Tbsp. light brown sugar
2 Tbsp. chili powder
2 Tbsp. smoked paprika
1 Tbsp. ground cumin
1½ tsp. freshly ground black pepper
1 tsp. ground red pepper

RIBS

3 slabs baby back pork ribs
  (about 3 lb. each)
¼ cup vegetable oil
2 cups hickory chips
Habanero Barbecue Sauce

Habanero Barbecue Sauce

HANDS-ON 15 MIN.   TOTAL 45 MIN.

MAKES 2 CUPS

Bring first 7 ingredients to a boil in a medium saucepan over medium-high heat, stirring occasionally. Reduce heat to low, and simmer, stirring occasionally, 10 minutes. Pulse mixture with a handheld blender until smooth, being sure that no small pieces or chunks remain. (If you don't have a handheld blender, process in a regular blender until smooth. Return mixture to saucepan, and proceed with recipe.) Stir in brown sugar and ketchup. Simmer mixture over medium-low heat, stirring occasionally, 30 minutes or until slightly thickened and blended. Serve immediately, or cool sauce to room temperature, and refrigerate in an airtight container until ready to use; reheat sauce before serving.

INGREDIENTS

¼ cups apple cider vinegar
½ Vidalia or sweet onion, coarsely chopped
1 habanero pepper, halved lengthwise
  and seeded
½ jalapeño pepper, halved lengthwise
  and seeded
2 garlic cloves, minced
¾ tsp. kosher salt
½ tsp. freshly ground black pepper
¾ cup firmly packed light brown sugar
½ cup ketchup

Cast-Iron Pork Tenderloin + Blackberry Bourbon Barbecue Sauce

This is one of my go-to dishes whenever blackberries are in season. In college, I spent a summer working at the Georgia Seed Plant with my friends Tom Seward, Josh Counce, and Kirk Alexander. We rogued wheat fields, cleaned combines, and packed up feed and seed for the US Department of Agriculture. It was tough work, but the camaraderie got us through.

We also cut the grass, and I volunteered for the front lawn, though it meant more work. I had a little secret—a blackberry bush stood on the east end of the property. With each lap, I'd grab a handful of fresh berries to eat to cool off from the summer heat. This recipe always takes me back to those times, with its sweet, tangy barbecue sauce paired with this juicy, tender pork tenderloin.

HANDS-ON 20 MIN. **TOTAL 35 MIN.**
SERVES 4

⇒ INGREDIENTS ⇐

1 Tbsp. extra virgin olive oil
1 (1¼) lb. pork tenderloin
1 tsp. kosher salt
¾ tsp. freshly ground black pepper
1½ cups fresh blackberries
¼ cup molasses
¼ cup ketchup
1 Tbsp. plus 1½ tsp. whole grain mustard
1 Tbsp. red wine vinegar
1 Tbsp. Kentucky bourbon
Pinch of kosher salt
½ tsp. hot sauce

1 Preheat oven to 425°. Drizzle oil over tenderloin, and sprinkle with salt and pepper.

2 Pulse blackberries and next 7 ingredients in a blender or food processor until mixture is fully blended and smooth. Transfer mixture to a small saucepan, and cook over medium-low heat, stirring occasionally, 10 minutes or until slightly thickened. Strain out blackberry seeds, if desired.

3 Meanwhile, place a 12-inch cast-iron skillet over medium-high heat 1 minute or until hot. Add pork, and cook 2 minutes on each side or until browned. Transfer skillet to oven. Bake pork at 425° for 8-10 minutes or until a meat thermometer inserted into thickest portion registers 145°. Transfer pork to a cutting board, and cover loosely with aluminum foil; let stand 5 minutes.

4 Cut pork diagonally across the grain into ½-inch-thick slices. Serve with warm blackberry sauce.

Summer at the Georgia Seed Plant

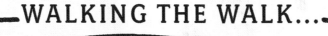

THE BOAR HUNT

Bow and arrow? Check. Camouflage? Check. Flying into virgin hunting grounds strapped in the seat of an MD 600 helicopter? Check. These are just some of the manly pursuits one can enjoy while spending time on the Franklin Ranch just outside Osteen, Florida. Owner Greg Arnette (the same dude who created Arnette sunglasses) has created an 8,000-acre paradise for those seeking to kill a wild boar. Let me tell you, there's nothing more exciting than standing 20 yards away from one of these wild beasts with just a bow in hand.

Fortunately our group was quite lucky during our visit, and we landed a boar just before dusk to cook up for evening supper. Since wild boar is not native to the region, and it's also a nuisance to wildlife and agriculture, hunting is highly encouraged—and that goes for eating, too.

Wild Boar Chops

Due to the natural leanness of the meat, I like to brine my boar chops in a simple solution, which ensures that they will stay moist and juicy. From there, I grill the chops over an open flame until they reach a perfect medium doneness. Carolina-style, I pair them with a mustard-based barbecue sauce that packs sweetness and heat, and acidity, making these boar chops the envy of everyone on the ranch.

HANDS-ON 37 MIN. **TOTAL 3 HR., 42 MIN.**
SERVES 10

1 Prepare Brine and Chops: Combine first 4 ingredients in a large plastic bowl, stirring until salt and sugar dissolve. Stir in ice until melted. Add chops to brine mixture; cover and chill 3-24 hours. Remove chops from brine, and pat dry with paper towels; discard brine. Let stand at room temperature 30 minutes.

2 Meanwhile, light 1 side of grill, heating to 350°-400° (medium-high); leave other side unlit. Sprinkle both sides of chops with ½ tsp. salt and ½ tsp. pepper. Place chops over lit side of grill, and grill, covered with grill lid, 4 minutes. Rotate chops 45°, and grill, covered with grill lid, 5 more minutes to create grill marks. Turn chops over while transferring to unlit side of grill; grill chops, covered with grill lid, 14-18 minutes or until a meat thermometer inserted in thickest portion registers 145°. Remove chops from grill; cover loosely with aluminum foil, and let stand 5 minutes.

3 Meanwhile, prepare Sauce: Combine mustard and next 4 ingredients in a medium-size heavy saucepan with metal handle, and place over lit side of grill. Bring to a simmer. Transfer pan to unlit side of grill, and cook, stirring occasionally, 8 minutes or until mixture thickens.

4 Spoon a generous amount of sauce on 1 side of each serving plate, and move spoon in a quick, smooth motion to thinly spread sauce across the plate. Place 1 chop in center of sauce for each serving. Serve immediately.

⇒ BRINE AND CHOPS ⇐

½ gallon warm water
½ cup kosher salt
½ cup firmly packed light brown sugar
2 bay leaves
4 cups ice cubes
10 (10- to 12-oz.) double-cut bone-in wild boar chops with bones frenched, trimmed (2 racks)
½ tsp. kosher salt
½ tsp. freshly ground black pepper

⇒ SAUCE ⇐

1 cup whole grain mustard
¼ cup firmly packed light brown sugar
⅓ cup apple cider vinegar
1 Tbsp. Worcestershire sauce
½ tsp. ground red pepper

Whole Roasted Hog

The day you decide to roast a whole hog...that, my friends, is a day worth celebrating. There are several methods for preparing a whole hog. I use a large grill/smoker because it can maintain a steady temperature of 225°. My cooking is truly an event so I like to use hardwood embers to add smoky, subtle flavor. Plan to use a half-cord of wood to keep the fire burning all evening. You'll use the burning embers from the fire to cook the hog. If that feels like too much work, use about 75 lbs. lump charcoal. Notice I said *lump* charcoal and not charcoal briquettes—do not use briquettes, otherwise I will drive to your pig roast and settle this disgrace accordingly.

HANDS-ON 1 HR., NOT INCLUDING TENDING THE FIRE **TOTAL 16 HR., 30 MIN.**

SERVES 75-100

⇒ HOG ⇐

1 (125-lb.) fully dressed whole hog
½ cord of hardwood

⇒ RUB ⇐

6 cups kosher salt
3 cups packed light brown sugar
2 cups ground black pepper
1 cup smoked paprika
1 cup garlic powder
1 cup ground cumin
1 cup chili powder
½ cup ground red pepper
1 gallon extra virgin olive oil
Heavy-duty aluminum foil

⇒ DOUSE LIQUID ⇐

1 gallon apple cider vinegar
½ cup dried crushed red pepper

Garnish: apple

1 Afternoon, day before party: Set up grill and party area—lay out chairs and coolers, clear space for a large fire, etc. You'll want to have setup completed before beginning your work on the hog, which will require your utmost attention for the next 15 hours.

2 Pre-dusk, day before party: Pick up the hog and supplies the day before the party. Keep the hog cold in a large cooler. Light the fire using hardwood. Prepare Rub. Whisk together kosher salt and next 7 ingredients in a large bowl, stirring with a fork to break apart any clumps and blend ingredients thoroughly. Prepare Pig. Remove hog from cooler, and pat completely dry with paper towels. Rub entire hog, including cavity, generously with olive oil. Sprinkle Rub over hog and in cavity, rubbing until thoroughly coated. Shield ears and nose of hog with heavy-duty aluminum foil to prevent excessive browning. Place hog, cavity side down, on cold cooking grate of a large grill, adjusting so hog is as flat as possible.

3 Dusk, day before party: Crack open a cold beer, and turn on some tunes. Add about 10 lb. hot wood embers from fire to bed of grill using a shovel. Cover grill, and open vents to allow air to flow properly. Heat grill to an internal temperature of 225°. Prepare Douse Liquid. Combine vinegar and dried crushed red pepper in a large mixing bowl or bucket. Once grill reaches 225°, transfer hog on cooking grate to grill, and grill, covered with grill lid, 15 hours or until a meat thermometer inserted into the hind quarter registers 160°, dousing entire hog every hour. Continue to burn wood via a fire so that you can continue to add hot embers from the fire to the grill every hour or so during grilling time to maintain 225°. (Note: **DO NOT GO TO SLEEP!** A larger group can work in shifts, if necessary, but you will miss all the fun.)

4 Morning of party: Remove hog from grill; cover entire hog loosely with foil, and let stand 1 to 2 hours. Take a nap. Remove foil just before serving.

5 Party time: Serve hog, inviting guests use their hands to dig in and tear off pieces of crispy skin and juicy, tender meat—nothing is more primal. For a more formal approach, present the whole hog to your guests (placing the apple in the hog's mouth and maybe putting some sunglasses on it). Then chop or pull meat from hog so that guests can use utensils to serve themselves. Serve with cold beer, toasted buns, assorted barbecue sauces, and desired sides.

Cooking + Family

Beef kabobs were a weekly supper in my family. Mama would make up a batch of these early in the morning and let them sit, marinating all day. When suppertime came around, Ashley and I often helped skewer the meat and vegetables, while Dad maintained close watch over the grill. To me, that's the essence of a family meal—each member pitching in to do his or her part to share in the goodness.

Tender Beef Kabobs + Tzatziki

I can always remember the unique flavor of this dish, which is due mainly to Mama's traditional Lebanese-style marinade that included mint, allspice, and cinnamon. It just doesn't get any better than that. I pair this up with a homemade tzatziki sauce to really set this meal over the top.

HANDS-ON 22 MIN. TOTAL 8 HR., 25 MIN.

SERVES 4

1 Smash garlic using the flat side of a knife. Combine smashed garlic and next 5 ingredients in a large zip-top plastic freezer bag; add steak pieces and next 6 ingredients, turning to coat. Seal and chill for 3-24 hours.

2 Soak wooden skewers in water 30 min. Preheat grill to 300°-350° (medium).

3 Remove beef and vegetables from marinade, discarding marinade. Thread beef and vegetables alternately onto skewers, leaving ¼-inch space between pieces.

4 Grill kabobs, covered with grill lid, 2-3 minutes on each side (medium-rare) or to desired degree of doneness. Remove from grill, and let stand 5 minutes before serving. Serve with Tzatziki.

⊰ INGREDIENTS ⊱

10 garlic cloves
½ cup extra virgin olive oil
¼ cup balsamic vinegar
2 Tbsp. red wine vinegar
2 Tbsp. fresh lemon juice
2 Tbsp. chopped fresh mint
2 lb. top sirloin steaks, cut into
  20 (1½-inch) pieces
1 large red onion, quartered
2 medium green bell peppers,
  cut into 1½-inch pieces
2 Tbsp. kosher salt
1 Tbsp. freshly ground black pepper
1 tsp. ground allspice
¼ tsp. ground cinnamon
Wooden skewers

Tzatziki

HANDS-ON 3 MIN. TOTAL 3 MIN.

MAKES 1¾ CUPS

1 Whisk together all ingredients in a bowl. Serve immediately, or cover and chill until ready to serve. May be made up to 1 day ahead; refrigerate it in an airtight container.

⊰ INGREDIENTS ⊱

1 cup plain Greek yogurt
1 Tbsp. minced garlic
½ cucumber, peeled, seeded,
  and finely grated
1½ tsp. fresh lemon juice
¼ tsp. kosher salt

Recession Special Red Beans + Rice

Back in the Great Recession of 2008, my favorite honky-tonk, Robert's in Nashville's historic Lower Broadway district, ran a great deal. The "Recession Special" cost just $5, and consisted of a fried bologna sandwich, a bag of Lay's original potato chips, an ice-cold Pabst Blue Ribbon, and your choice between either a Goo Goo Cluster or a MoonPie. Back in my single days, my crew—Tex, Krones, Chris, Bobby, Robert, Miller, and I sure did eat a lot of those Recession Specials. The best part about Robert's wasn't the food—it was the incredible Western swing and traditional music that was played from 10 a.m. till 2 a.m. daily, not to mention the cute girls. Heaven. On. Earth.

Of course, a meal such as the Recession Special wasn't always the healthiest of choices. Nevertheless, sometimes the tastiest meals are those that require the least amount of ingredients, like my own recession special of rice and beans. Let's be clear, I've eaten many a plate of rice and beans, so this is one recipe I've definitely perfected on the cheap! You can also make this recipe vegetarian-friendly by cutting out the ham—either way, it's a real pleaser.

HANDS-ON 35 MIN. TOTAL 10 HR., 35 MIN.

SERVES 8

≷ INGREDIENTS ≶

- 1 (16-oz.) package dried red kidney beans
- 2 Tbsp. extra virgin olive oil
- 1 lb. tasso ham or 1 (16-oz.) ham steak, diced
- 1 large Vidalia or sweet onion, finely diced
- ½ cup finely diced green bell pepper
- 2 celery ribs, finely diced
- 1 Tbsp. Creole seasoning
- 3 garlic cloves, minced
- 8 cups chicken stock
- 4 cups hot cooked rice
- Garnish: sliced green onions

1 Place beans in a large bowl, and cover with water to 2 inches above beans. Let soak 8-24 hours; drain.

2 Place a Dutch oven over medium-high heat 1 minute or until hot; add oil. Cook ham in hot oil, stirring occasionally, 5 minutes or just until browned. Add onion and next 3 ingredients, and sauté 8 minutes or just until vegetables are tender. Add garlic, and sauté 1 minute or just until fragrant.

3 Stir in beans and stock. Bring to a light boil over medium-high heat; reduce heat to medium-low, and simmer, stirring occasionally, 2 hours or until beans are tender.

4 Serve bean mixture in shallow bowls. Top with hot cooked rice.

Grilled Hot Dogs with Aunt Mary's Relish + Sweet Potato Fries

In my opinion, the proper way to cook a hot dog is directly over a charcoal fire—cooking the dog until heated through, slightly charred, and just about to bust at the seams. Such a method creates a smoky, perfectly cooked dog that only gets better when liberally topped with Aunt Mary's relish.

HANDS-ON 23 MIN. TOTAL 50 MIN.

SERVES 4

AUNT MARY'S RELISH

3 plum tomatoes, seeded and finely diced
¼ cup finely diced Vidalia or sweet onion
¼ tsp. kosher salt
½ tsp. freshly ground black pepper
1½ Tbsp. yellow mustard

SWEET POTATO FRIES

2 sweet potatoes (about 2 lb.)
2 Tbsp. extra virgin olive oil
1 Tbsp. fresh lemon juice
1 tsp. kosher salt
1 tsp. light brown sugar
¼ tsp. ground cinnamon
¼ tsp. ground red pepper

HOT DOGS

4 beef hot dogs
4 hot dog buns

1 Preheat oven to 425°. Prepare Aunt Mary's Relish: Stir together tomatoes and next 4 ingredients in a serving bowl. Let relish stand at room temperature at least 5 minutes before serving. (To make ahead, cover and chill until ready to serve).

2 Prepare Sweet Potato Fries: Cut sweet potatoes in half lengthwise, and cut each half again lengthwise to create 4 pieces. Cut each lengthwise into 4 pieces, creating a total of 16 wedges per potato. Place fries on an ungreased baking sheet. Drizzle with oil and lemon juice; sprinkle with salt and next 3 ingredients. Toss fries with hands to season evenly. Arrange fries in a single layer, and bake at 425°, shaking pan occasionally, 35 minutes or until fries are tender.

3 Meanwhile, prepare Hot Dogs: Preheat grill to 300°-350° (medium). Grill hot dogs, without grill lid, turning frequently, 8 minutes or until hot dogs are thoroughly heated and slightly charred on all sides. Add buns to grill with hot dogs during last 1 minute and 30 seconds of grill time; grill buns, cut sides down, until toasted and grill marks appear.

4 Place hot dogs in toasted buns, and top with relish. Serve with fries.

Charcoal Perfection

These dogs are better than anything you'll get at the ballpark. My mama's Aunt Mary used to make this peppery tomato and onion relish to serve over charcoal-grilled hot dogs whenever the kids visited her home in Jacksonville, Florida. It's a recipe that has lasted for several generations in our family, and for me, it doesn't get any better than a simple dish like this. Perfect for a quick weeknight meal and paired up with the salty sweet combo of the fries, I can promise y'all are in for some good eatin'.

"Coke" is the preferred default term for all soft drinks throughout most of the South. If you request a Coke at a local restaurant, the waiter is likely to follow with, "What flavor?" To which we'd commonly answer Classic, Dr Pepper®, Sprite®, or Cherry.

DRINK
Coca-Cola
IN BOTTLES

Grilled Flank Steak with Coca-Cola® Marinade

This beloved drink is not only great for refreshment, but it's also delicious when used as a tenderizer and marinade. Flank steak takes well to such a marinade—soaking up the salty and sweet flavors, and it also makes a real friendly, affordable dish for entertaining. I like to slice the meat thin, which allows me to control portion sizes and "stretch" the meal.

HANDS-ON 13 MIN. TOTAL 9 HR., 3 MIN.

SERVES 4

1 Combine first 5 ingredients in a small saucepan. Cook over medium-high heat 20 minutes or until reduced to 1 cup. Cool completely (about 30 minutes). Stir in green onions. Reserve ¼ cup marinade; cover and chill. Pour remaining ¾ cup marinade into a large zip-top plastic freezer bag; add flank steak, turning to coat. Seal bag, and chill 8 hours. Remove from refrigerator, and let stand at room temperature 30 minutes. Remove reserved ¼ cup marinade from refrigerator, and let stand at room temperature.

2 Meanwhile, preheat grill to 400°-450° (high). Remove steak from marinade, shaking off excess marinade; discard marinade in bag or see "Gent's Tip" below. Sprinkle with salt. Grill steak 4-5 minutes on each side or until a meat thermometer inserted into the thickest portion of steak registers 135° (medium-rare).

3 Transfer steak to a cutting board; cover loosely with aluminum foil. Let stand 5 minutes. Cut steak diagonally across the grain into ¼-inch slices. Serve with reserved ¼ cup marinade.

⇒ INGREDIENTS ⇐

- 1 (12-oz.) can Coca-Cola® or other cola soft drink
- 2 Tbsp. soy sauce
- 1 Tbsp. honey
- 1 Tbsp. yellow mustard
- 1 tsp. freshly ground black pepper
- 2 Tbsp. chopped green onions
- 2 lb. flank steak
- ½ tsp. kosher salt

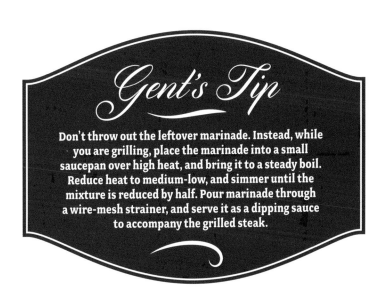

Gent's Tip

Don't throw out the leftover marinade. Instead, while you are grilling, place the marinade into a small saucepan over high heat, and bring it to a steady boil. Reduce heat to medium-low, and simmer until the mixture is reduced by half. Pour marinade through a wire-mesh strainer, and serve it as a dipping sauce to accompany the grilled steak.

JEFF FRANCOEUR

You will never meet a more driven, competitive person than Jeff Francoeur. That said, the same guy who's got you huffing and puffing on the athletic field, while running circles around you (and running his mouth), just so happens to be one of the finest gentleman on the planet. I should know. I've been competing against Jeff since tee-ball.

Long before Jeff was touted as "The Natural" while gracing the front cover of *Sports Illustrated*, he was just another kid growing up in our hometown of Lilburn, Georgia. In those days, our dads would coach our Dixie Youth baseball teams, teaching us the fundamentals of America's pastime, the pride of victory, and the sting of loss. To this day, Jeff and I still argue over whose team won the minor league championship.

In high school, we were fortunate to finally play on the same team. Those competitive early years created a fortified team, resulting in undefeated seasons and state championships in both baseball and football. Of course, all those workouts, practices, and games made us some hearty eaters too—Jeff included.

Upon signing a multi-million dollar contract with the Braves, Frenchie, as he was nicknamed, was thrust into the national spotlight. As always, Jeff met the call of duty—his rookie year still ranks amongst the best in MLB history.

After nearly ten years in the league, Jeff has seen it all—success, adversity, injuries, trades, and acclaim. His journey in the league is testament to the beauty of the game of baseball. Sir Thomas Carlyle once said "gunpowder makes all men alike tall." I would argue, "professional baseball makes all men alike human." Let me restate that in my southern slang—the game of baseball ain't easy. Nevertheless, Jeff has prevailed.

In recent years, the press has caught on to what we've always known, referring to Jeff as "the nicest guy in baseball." Beloved by fans, feared by competitors, and still a guy that you just want to enjoy a post-game whiskey with at the bar, Jeff's greatest accomplishment, beyond the Golden Gloves and national praise, is the proven reality that good guys finish first.

Be honest. Lead with generosity. Remain steadfast and faithful. Above all else, smile ear-to-ear. Those are the qualities I admire most about Jeff Francoeur.

And food? You can bet that Jeff enjoys a big meal of Meat 'n' Potatoes after those long games and off-season workouts. Fortunately, Jeff's high-school sweetheart, and just as admirable wife Catie, has let me in on the fact that even after all these years traversing coast-to-coast and having his pick of the finest restaurants, Jeff is still simply a meat 'n' potatoes kind of guy.

I can't promise that eating this meal will make you into a famous athlete, but if it comes close to embodying the character of this man, you are likely on your way to greatness.

Meat 'n' Potatoes

The name might be simple, but I've gussied up this classic pairing with a perfectly cooked New York strip steak and a hearty garlic mash. The key is rendering the side fat prior to searing the steak in a skillet then finishing it in the oven. I baste the steak with the rendered fat and butter throughout, resulting in a deliciously tender, juicy steak.

HANDS-ON 23 MIN. TOTAL 1 HR., 33 MIN.

SERVES 4

1 Let steaks stand at room temperature 30 minutes. Preheat oven to 400°. Cut off, and discard pointed end of garlic; place garlic on a piece of aluminum foil, and drizzle with oil. Fold foil to seal, and bake 40 minutes. Remove from foil, and cool 15 minutes. Squeeze pulp from garlic into a bowl.

2 Bring potatoes, 1 tsp. salt, and cold water to cover to a boil in a large saucepan over high heat; cook 10 minutes or until fork-tender. Drain, allowing potatoes to steam to prevent them from becoming watery. Meanwhile, cook ½ cup butter, milk, and garlic pulp in same saucepan over low heat 2 minutes or until butter melts and mixture is thoroughly heated. Return potatoes to saucepan, add pepper and 1 tsp. salt; mash with a potato masher to desired consistency. Cover and keep warm.

3 Place a 12-inch cast-iron skillet over medium-high heat 4 minutes or until hot. (Be sure kitchen is well ventilated.) Make ¼-inch-deep cuts in fat on long side of each steak with a sharp knife. Place steaks, fat sides down, in hot skillet, and cook 2 minutes or until fat is golden brown. Turn steaks to meaty side, and cook 1 minute or until seared. Turn steaks over, and top seared side of each steak with 1 Tbsp. of remaining butter. Cook 3-4 minutes or to desired degree of doneness; spoon pan drippings over steaks. Remove steaks from skillet; sprinkle both sides of steaks with remaining ½ tsp. salt, and let stand 5 minutes before serving with mashed potatoes.

INGREDIENTS

4 (6-oz.) beef strip or shell steaks
1 garlic bulb
1 Tbsp. extra virgin olive oil
3 lb. small red potatoes, quartered
2½ tsp. kosher salt, divided
¾ cup unsalted butter, divided
½ cup milk
½ tsp. freshly ground black pepper
Garnish: finely chopped fresh parsley

Pan-Seared Skirt Steak + Chimichurri

Traditionally used as fajita meat, skirt steak is gaining popularity these days as a stand-alone meat. It's my preferred cut of beef because it offers great flavor, tenderness, and affordability.

I like to pan-sear this all-in-one cut over really high heat in my cast-iron skillet to create a nice char on the outside of the meat (open a window or turn on the fan in the kitchen). Instead of wasting time on a marinade, I prefer to reverse the process by slicing the meat thin and pouring all of the chimichurri sauce over the meat prior to serving. Trust me, it's a real showstopper when it comes to entertaining. Even better, this chimichurri sauce is super versatile. It also goes well on pork, chicken, and firm cuts of fish, such as shark and swordfish.

HANDS-ON 21 MIN.   TOTAL 26 MIN.

SERVES 6

1 Place a 12-inch cast-iron skillet over medium-high heat 2-3 minutes or until hot. Coat steak with 2 Tbsp. oil, and season both sides of steak with 1½ tsp. salt and 1 tsp. pepper. Cook steak in hot skillet 3-4 minutes on each side or until a meat thermometer inserted into thickest portion registers 130° (medium-rare). Transfer steak to a cutting board, and cover loosely with aluminum foil; let stand 5 minutes.

2 Meanwhile, make chimichurri by stirring together onion, garlic, remaining 1 tsp. salt, and remaining 1 tsp. pepper in a small bowl. Stir in vinegar; let stand 5 minutes. Stir in parsley. Add remaining ¾ cup oil in a slow, steady stream, whisking constantly until smooth.

3 Cut steak diagonally across grain into ¼-inch-thick slices, and place on a serving platter. Pour chimichurri over sliced steak, and serve immediately.

⇉ INGREDIENTS ⇇

2 lb. skirt steak

¾ cup plus 2 Tbsp. extra virgin olive oil, divided

2½ tsp. kosher salt, divided

2 tsp. freshly ground black pepper, divided

¼ cup finely chopped red onion

2 large garlic cloves, minced

¼ cup red wine vinegar

½ cup chopped fresh parsley

Fajitas and 'Ritas

Honestly, there's nothing better than a full-on fajita and margarita party in a springtime backyard filled with good friends. While waiting for the feast, I serve guests a big ole batch of my stiff margs, while providing album after album of the Randy Rogers Band as my soundtrack. The reason I like this kind of party is that it's reasonable from a cost perspective. I supplement my tasty recipes with huge trays of cooked refried beans and Spanish rice to keep everything on budget, not to mention providing each of my guests with a full belly to keep things from getting too out of control! Like any hosted party, I recommend prepping as much as possible a day or so in advance.

HANDS-ON **1 HR., 11 MIN.** TOTAL **1 HR., 11 MIN.,** PLUS 1 DAY FOR MARINATING

SERVES **15**

⇒ INGREDIENTS ⇐

6 limes
15 garlic cloves
5 cups canola oil
¼ cup red wine vinegar
¼ cup Worcestershire sauce
3 jalapeño peppers, cut in half lengthwise
¼ cup kosher salt
¼ cup ground cumin
¼ cup chili powder
2 Tbsp. sugar
5 lb. skirt steak
5 lb. skinned and boned chicken breasts
5 medium red onions, cut in half
5 medium green bell peppers, cut in half and seeded
5 medium yellow bell peppers, cut in half and seeded
30 (10-inch) burrito-size flour tortillas
Toppings: sour cream, guacamole, pico de gallo
Classic Margaritas

1 Squeeze juice from limes into a measuring cup to equal 6 Tbsp., reserving limes. Smash garlic cloves using flat side of a knife. Combine lime juice, reserved limes, smashed garlic, oil, and next 7 ingredients in a large bowl. Divide mixture among 3 large zip-top plastic freezer bags. Add steak, chicken, and vegetables each to its own bag of marinade to prevent cross-contamination. Seal bags, and chill 24 hours.

2 Preheat grill to 350°-400° (medium-high). Meanwhile, remove steak, chicken, and vegetables from marinade, shaking off any excess; discard marinade in bags. Grill chicken and vegetables at the same time, covered with grill lid. Grill chicken 6-8 minutes on each side or until done; grill vegetables, turning occasionally, 12-16 minutes or until vegetables are charred and tender. Transfer chicken and vegetables to a large plate, cover with aluminum foil, and keep warm.

3 Grill steak 4-5 minutes on each side or until a meat thermometer inserted in thickest portion registers 135° (medium rare). Transfer steak to a large cutting board, cover with foil, and let stand 5-8 minutes. Thinly slice steak, chicken, and vegetables.

4 Grill tortillas 30 seconds on each side or until warm and lightly charred; keep tortillas warm. Add half of sliced vegetables to chicken and remaining vegetables to steak. Serve chicken mixture and steak mixture in tortillas with toppings and Classic Margaritas.

CLASSIC MARGARITA

HANDS-ON **5 MIN.** TOTAL **5 MIN.**

SERVES **1**

≥ INGREDIENTS ≤

Lime wedge

Kosher salt

½ cup silver or blanco tequila

¼ cup fresh lime juice

2 Tbsp. orange liqueur

1 Tbsp. light agave nectar

1 pasteurized egg white

1 Rub rim of a chilled margarita glass with lime wedge; dip rim of glass in salt to coat. Combine tequila and next 4 ingredients in a cocktail shaker; add ice. Cover with lid, and shake vigorously until thoroughly blended (about 30 seconds). Strain into prepared glass, and serve immediately.

Green Pea + Portobello Mushroom Risotto

The key to making any great risotto is love and attention. With constant stirring, you allow the natural starches in the rice to develop into a creamy, rich base. You'll need to be on standby and keep close watch over the dish, but that's what a glass of wine is for.

I also like the fact that this dish is vegetarian-friendly.

Since I serve a lot of dinner parties where I'm unsure of my guest's dietary needs, this is my go-to dish for satisfying all tastes and preferences, while leaving everyone feeling completely satisfied. The meaty portobello mushrooms add a good heft of texture to the creamy rice, and the sweet green peas add a nice pop of flavor and color.

HANDS-ON 1 HR., 2 MIN. TOTAL 1 HR., 2 MIN.

SERVES 4

1 Bring stock to a simmer in a large saucepan over medium-high heat. Reduce heat to low; gently simmer until ready to use.

2 Place a large skillet over medium-high heat 1 minute or until hot; add 2 Tbsp. oil. Add garlic and shallot, and sprinkle with ½ tsp. salt, ¼ tsp. black pepper, and, if desired, ¼ tsp. red pepper; sauté 2 minutes or until shallot is tender and garlic is fragrant. Add rice, and cook, stirring constantly, 2 minutes or until rice begins to look opaque. Add wine, and cook, stirring to loosen any browned bits from bottom of skillet, 1 minute.

3 Reduce heat to medium; add 1 cup warm stock, and cook, stirring constantly with a wooden spoon, until liquid is absorbed. Repeat procedure with remaining stock, 1 cup at a time, until liquid is absorbed and rice is al dente and creamy (all of the stock may not be used). Total cooking time is 25-30 minutes. Stir in green peas, and cook 2 minutes or until thoroughly heated.

4 Add butter, ¼ cup cream, and ¼ cup cheese, and cook, stirring vigorously, until blended and smooth; add more cream, if needed, to ensure mixture is creamy. (Risotto should spread, not stand, when spooned onto a plate.) Cover and keep warm.

5 Place a 12-inch cast-iron skillet over medium-high heat 1 minute or until hot; add remaining 1 Tbsp. oil. Add mushrooms; sprinkle with remaining ½ tsp. salt and remaining ¼ tsp. black pepper, and sauté 4 minutes or until mushroom slices are softened and tender.

6 Spoon risotto into center of shallow bowls; top with sautéed mushrooms, and sprinkle with fresh basil and desired amount of grated Parmigiano-Reggiano cheese. Serve immediately.

⋛ INGREDIENTS ⋚

6 cups vegetable stock

3 Tbsp. extra virgin olive oil, divided

2 garlic cloves, minced

1 shallot, minced

1 tsp. kosher salt, divided

½ tsp. freshly ground black pepper, divided

¼ tsp. dried crushed red pepper (optional)

1 cup uncooked Arborio rice

½ cup dry white wine

1 cup fresh green peas*

2 Tbsp. unsalted butter

¼ cup heavy cream

¼ cup (1 oz.) grated Parmigiano-Reggiano cheese

3 (8-oz.) packages portobello mushroom caps, cleaned and cut into ⅓-inch slices

1 Tbsp. finely chopped fresh basil

Grated Parmigiano-Reggiano cheese

*Frozen green peas, thawed, may be substituted.

Tuesday Night Lights

There's a reason this dish was served on Tuesdays at my house. When I was in high school, I spent the hours from 2:45 until 8 p.m. on the football fields running plays until our coach, Cecil Flowe, decided he'd had enough. To my knowledge, Parkview High was the only school in the state of Georgia that had lights on its practice fields. Those lights got used many a night, especially on Tuesdays when playoff season came around. Fortunately our hard work paid off in the form of an undefeated season and state championship title. Such long, enduring practices were always made better knowing that Mama had this comforting dish sitting ready for me in a warm skillet.

Tuesday Night Hamburger Steak

This hearty meal always eased the pain of running Oklahoma drills well into the evening. Most often, Mama would serve this with whipped potatoes and green beans, both of which I'd drown in the thick, savory gravy. I stayed healthy throughout the season, so I like to think that the steady dose of vitamins and minerals from the red meat, veggies, and cast-iron pan played a hand in putting that state championship ring on my finger.

HANDS-ON **46 MIN.** TOTAL **46 MIN.**

SERVES **4**

1 Shape meat with hands into 4 (3-inch) patties (each about ¾-inch thick). Season both sides of patties with 1 tsp. salt, ½ tsp. pepper, and garlic powder.

2 Place a 12-inch cast-iron skillet over medium heat 1 minute or until hot. Add patties, and cook 4 minutes on each side. Transfer patties to a plate, reserving drippings in skillet.

3 Add oil to reserved drippings in skillet, and cook over medium heat until hot. Add onion, mushrooms, and remaining ½ tsp. salt and ½ tsp. pepper; sauté 8 minutes or until onion is slightly browned and tender.

4 Sprinkle flour over onion mixture. Cook, stirring constantly with a wooden spoon, 1 minute or until flour is thoroughly blended and smooth. Slowly stir in beef stock, stirring to loosen browned bits from bottom of skillet. Stir in Worcestershire sauce, and bring mixture to a light boil, stirring constantly.

5 Reduce heat to medium-low, add patties to skillet, and simmer 10 minutes or until patties are thoroughly cooked and gravy thickens. Place patties on individual serving plates, and top each with gravy.

≥ INGREDIENTS ≤

1 lb. ground chuck
1½ tsp. kosher salt, divided
1 tsp. freshly ground black pepper, divided
½ tsp. garlic powder
1 Tbsp. extra virgin olive oil
1 medium Vidalia or sweet onion, coarsely chopped
1 (8-oz.) package fresh mushrooms, quartered
2 Tbsp. all-purpose flour
1¼ cups beef stock
Dash of Worcestershire sauce
Garnish: finely chopped fresh parsley

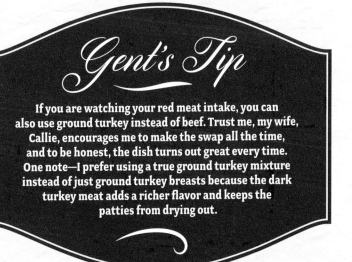

Gent's Tip

If you are watching your red meat intake, you can also use ground turkey instead of beef. Trust me, my wife, Callie, encourages me to make the swap all the time, and to be honest, the dish turns out great every time. One note—I prefer using a true ground turkey mixture instead of just ground turkey breasts because the dark turkey meat adds a richer flavor and keeps the patties from drying out.

Classic Southern Meatloaf

If you ever need or want something from me, your odds of getting a "yes" are a lot better after serving up this meal. Meatloaf is a cheap, filling crowd-pleaser that evokes savory comfort in every bite. When I was growing up, my family ate this with hot white rice and either collards or green beans as a side dish. Such a dinner was always delicious, but the leftovers always garnered my greatest attention in the form of a meatloaf sandwich.

I've written this recipe to ensure that there are plenty of leftovers for lunch the following day. Just reheat any remaining meatloaf, slice it as thick as you like, and sandwich it between two slices of white bread—mayo or cheese is optional—and you'll be as full as a tick on a bloodhound.

HANDS-ON 12 MIN. TOTAL **1 HR., 2 MIN.**

SERVES 4

⇒ INGREDIENTS ⇐

Vegetable cooking spray
2 white bread slices, crusts removed
½ cup milk
1½ lb. ground chuck
½ medium Vidalia or sweet onion, grated
1 garlic clove, minced
1 large egg, lightly beaten
1 tsp. kosher salt
½ tsp. freshly ground black pepper
2 Tbsp. finely chopped fresh parsley
¾ cup ketchup
1 tsp. whole grain mustard
1 Tbsp. plus 1½ tsp. soy sauce

1 Preheat oven to 375°. Lightly grease a 13- x 9-inch baking dish with cooking spray. Combine bread and milk in a large bowl, and let stand 5 minutes. Add meat and next 6 ingredients; combine mixture using hands and being careful not to overwork meat. Shape mixture into a 12- x 4-inch loaf, and place in baking dish.

2 Bake at 375° for 30 minutes.

3 Meanwhile, stir together ketchup, mustard, and soy sauce in a small bowl. Remove meatloaf from oven, and drain. Spread ketchup mixture over meatloaf. Bake 15 more minutes or until a meat thermometer inserted into thickest portion registers 165°. Remove from oven, and let stand 5 minutes before slicing and serving.

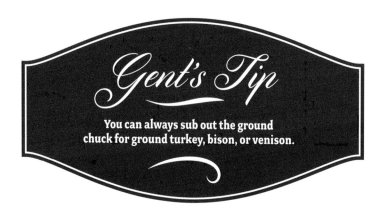

Gent's Tip

You can always sub out the ground chuck for ground turkey, bison, or venison.

Pasta Bolognese

On nights when I might be in the doghouse and I'm looking to impress my wife, Callie, I go with this meal. There's something incredibly rich and comforting about this simple dish. It won't wow you with presentation or complicated ingredients. In fact, it's just the opposite—warm, savory, and filling. It just radiates love in every single bite, and Callie always tends to forgive me when I serve it up.

If you don't have time to whip up a batch of Fresh Pappardelle Pasta, you can substitute a store-bought or dry version. For those looking to cut carbs, I recommend serving this over thinly sliced, quickly sautéed zucchini ribbons. Just use a vegetable peeler to slice the zucchini extra thin, pat dry with paper towels, and sauté for a minute or so in extra virgin olive oil.

HANDS-ON 29 MIN.   TOTAL 1 HR., 34 MIN.

SERVES 6

1 Place a Dutch oven over medium-high heat 2 minutes or until hot; add 1 Tbsp. oil. Add pancetta, ground chuck, and ground pork; cook, stirring occasionally, 7 minutes or until meat crumbles and is no longer pink. Remove meat from Dutch oven, and drain well.

2 Reduce heat to medium, and add remaining 1 Tbsp. oil to hot Dutch oven. Add onion and next 5 ingredients; sauté vegetable mixture 6 minutes or until onion is tender and translucent. Add garlic, and sauté just until fragrant. Push vegetable mixture to edges of Dutch oven, and add tomato paste to center; cook, stirring occasionally, 3 minutes or until it begins to bubble and char. Add red wine, and cook, stirring with a wooden spoon to loosen any browned bits from bottom of Dutch oven, 1 minute. Add tomatoes, and bring mixture to a simmer; cook 10 minutes.

3 Stir in cooked meat; cover, reduce heat to low, and simmer 55 minutes. Remove and discard bay leaves. Add nutmeg and cream, stirring until well blended. Serve over hot cooked Fresh Pappardelle Pasta.

⇒ INGREDIENTS ⇐

2 Tbsp. extra virgin olive oil, divided
¼ cup finely diced pancetta
1 lb. ground chuck or sirloin
1 lb. ground pork
1 large Vidalia or sweet onion, finely diced
2 carrots, grated (1 cup)
1½ tsp. kosher salt
1 tsp. freshly ground black pepper
2 bay leaves
1 tsp. dried oregano
4 garlic cloves, minced
1 (6-oz.) can tomato paste
2 cups dry red wine
1 (14.5-oz.) can petite diced tomatoes
¼ tsp. ground nutmeg
½ cup heavy cream
Fresh Pappardelle Pasta (page 172)*
Garnishes: finely chopped fresh flat-leaf parsley, freshly grated Parmigiano-Reggiano cheese

*16 oz. refrigerated fettuccine or linguine, prepared according to package directions, may be substituted.

Fresh Pappardelle Pasta

As it is, I went "old school" with this recipe, which serves as the perfect base to my Pasta Bolognese (page 171). Trust me—make this once, and you'll never go back to dried pasta again!

HANDS-ON **31 MIN.**   TOTAL **1 HR., 31 MIN.**

MAKES **6 CUPS**

⋟ INGREDIENTS ⋞

3¼ cups all-purpose flour, divided
6 large eggs, at room temperature
3 tsp. extra virgin olive oil, divided
Kosher salt

1 Place 2¾ cups flour in a large bowl, and make a very large well in center of flour. Add eggs and 2 tsp. oil to center of well. Gradually beat eggs and oil with a fork, stirring egg mixture into flour until a dough forms.

2 Turn dough out onto a lightly floured surface; knead dough by pushing away from your body with heel of your hand, folding dough onto itself, and turn clockwise, gradually adding up to ½ cup remaining flour to prevent dough from sticking to hands; continue kneading until dough is smooth and elastic (about 8 minutes). Tightly wrap dough in plastic wrap, and chill 1-24 hours.

3 Place dough on a lightly floured surface, and divide into 4 equal portions.

4 Using a lightly floured rolling pin, roll 1 dough portion to 1/16-inch thickness, working from center of dough to outside edge, and easing up in pressure as you reach edge. Dust with flour as needed to prevent sticking. (Dough should be transparent and thin.) Let dough stand 5 minutes.

5 Sprinkle rolled dough with flour, and fold in half. Repeat sprinkling and folding procedure until dough forms a cylinder shape (about 4 folds). Cut dough into 1-inch strips using a sharp knife. Unfold cut noodles, sprinkle with flour, and place on a baking sheet; cover noodles with a damp towel.

6 Repeat rolling and folding procedures in Steps 4 and 5 with remaining 3 dough portions.

7 Fill a large stockpot with water; heavily salt water with kosher salt, and stir in remaining 1 tsp. olive oil. Bring water to a rolling boil over high heat. Add pasta, and cook, stirring occasionally, 3 minutes or until al dente. Drain pasta, and serve immediately.

LAZZAROLI PASTA

I lived in Nashville's historic Germantown neighborhood, which sits within a foodie paradise a few blocks from the farmers' market, Little Brother's Seafood Company, and my personal favorite, Lazzaroli Pasta.

Tom Lazzaro makes homemade raviolis and pastas in his little market on 5th Avenue North—including a hefty supply of artisan and specialty goods, from salamis and cheeses to canned goods. I'd stop in nearly every Saturday to check-in with Tom, while sampling the array of his goods (see page 278). Tom and I agree that fresh pasta is something everyone needs in his or her culinary repertoire—no pasta machine or fancy equipment required, either.

Slow-Braised Beef + Parmesan Grits

Something magical occurs when you take tough, sinewy cuts of protein and cook them in liquid for long periods of time. The steady heat, moisture, and time produce tender, complex flavors in this dish that truly comfort the soul.

HANDS-ON 1 HR., 10 MIN. **TOTAL 4 HR., 10 MIN.**

SERVES 20

1 Prepare Beef: Preheat oven to 325°. Season chuck roast on all sides with 1 Tbsp. salt and 1½ tsp. pepper. Place a large Dutch oven over medium heat 1 minute or until hot; add 1 Tbsp. oil. Add roast, and cook 3 minutes on each side or until browned and a golden crust forms; transfer roast to a plate.

2 Add remaining 1 Tbsp. oil to Dutch oven. Add onions, celery, and carrots; sauté 5 minutes. Add garlic, and sauté 1½ minutes (be careful not to burn garlic). Push vegetable mixture to edges of Dutch oven, and add tomato paste to center. Cook tomato paste, stirring frequently, 2 minutes. Sprinkle flour over tomato paste and vegetable mixture; cook, stirring constantly, 2 minutes or until flour is blended into mixture. Add wine, and cook, stirring with a wooden spoon to loosen any browned bits from bottom of Dutch oven, 1 minute. Bring mixture to a light boil; reduce heat to medium-low, and simmer, stirring frequently, 8 minutes or until liquid is reduced by half. Return roast to Dutch oven, and place on vegetables. Add stock to Dutch oven (liquid should reach halfway up side of roast). Tie thyme sprigs into a bundle using kitchen string; add thyme bundle and bay leaves to Dutch oven; cover and transfer to oven. Bake at 325° for 2½ hours.

3 Place a large skillet over medium heat 1 minute or until hot; add butter, and cook 1 minute or until melted. Add mushrooms and pinch of salt; sauté 6-8 minutes or just until tender. Remove roast from oven, uncover, and stir in sautéed mushrooms. Bake, uncovered, 30 minutes or until liquid is slightly thickened.

4 Meanwhile, prepare Grits: Bring 3¼ cups water, 1 Tbsp. butter, and 1 tsp. salt to a boil over medium-high heat, stirring constantly. Gradually whisk in grits. Reduce heat to low, and cook, stirring occasionally, 30 minutes or until creamy and tender. Stir in cream and cheese until blended and cheese melts. Season with pepper and remaining ¼ tsp. salt.

5 Transfer roast to a plate; remove and discard thyme bundle and bay leaves, and reserve cooking liquid and vegetables in Dutch oven. Shred roast into bite-size pieces with 2 forks. Pour cooking liquid through a fine wire-mesh strainer into a bowl. Combine 3 cups strained cooking liquid, vegetables, and shredded roast, reserving remaining cooking liquid for another use. Spoon grits into large shallow bowls, and top with beef and vegetable mixture. Serve immediately.

Note: Tested with cremini, shiitake, and porcini mushrooms.

⇉ BEEF ⇇

1 (3-lb.) boneless beef chuck roast
1 Tbsp. kosher salt
1½ tsp. freshly ground black pepper
2 Tbsp. extra virgin olive oil, divided
2 medium Vidalia or sweet onions, quartered
3 celery ribs, coarsely chopped
5 carrots, coarsely chopped
3 garlic cloves, finely chopped
3 Tbsp. tomato paste
3 Tbsp. all-purpose flour
2 cups dry red wine
2 cups beef stock
10 fresh sprigs thyme
Kitchen string
2 bay leaves
3 Tbsp. unsalted butter
1 lb. assorted fresh mushrooms
Pinch of kosher salt
Garnish: finely chopped fresh parsley

⇉ GRITS ⇇

1 Tbsp. unsalted butter
1¼ tsp. kosher salt, divided
1 cup uncooked stone-ground grits
¾ cup heavy cream
1 cup (4 oz.) freshly grated Parmigiano-Reggiano cheese
¼ tsp. freshly ground black pepper

Slow-Roasted Beef + Carrots + Pan Gravy

Ah, yes, it doesn't get much better than this. Slow-roasted, tender beef immersed in flavorful pan gravy is the epitome of comfort cooking. Fair warning—the ingredient list might be minimal, but that's because you need a bit of time to let these flavorful ingredients work together to pull off such a magical dish.

This roast is best served alongside some sweet carrots, which cut the fatty flavor of the meat while lending a nice bright color to the dish. As an added bonus, the roast is studded with garlic cloves, which lend incredible essence into each and every bite.

Prep this dish in the early afternoon then allow it to roast away and "season" the house with great smells for a few hours until dinner rolls around. I can promise that such rich aromas will bring everyone to the family table before you can ring the dinner bell.

HANDS-ON 8 MIN.   TOTAL 3 HR., 58 MIN.

SERVES 8

⇒ INGREDIENTS ⇐

1 (3¾-lb.) boneless beef rump roast
8 garlic cloves
1 Tbsp. kosher salt
1 Tbsp. freshly ground black pepper
1 Tbsp. olive oil
2 medium Vidalia or sweet onions,
  coarsely chopped
2 cups dry red wine
10 carrots, trimmed
3 Tbsp. all-purpose flour
2 Tbsp. unsalted butter
2 Tbsp. finely chopped fresh flat-leaf
  parsley

1 Preheat oven to 325°. Place a Dutch oven over medium-high heat 2 minutes or until hot. Cut 8 slits in roast using a sharp knife; push a garlic clove into each slit. Sprinkle roast with salt and pepper.

2 Cook roast 2-3 minutes or until browned on each of 3 sides (do not cook on side with fat layer). Transfer roast to a plate. Add oil to Dutch oven; add onions, and sauté 3 minutes or until tender. Add wine, and cook, stirring with a wooden spoon to loosen any browned bits from bottom of Dutch oven, 30 seconds. Place roast on cooked onion, fat side up. Cover Dutch oven, and transfer to oven; bake roast, covered, at 325° for 2 hours.

3 Remove roast from oven. Add carrots, placing them around roast. Cover and bake 1 hour and 30 minutes or until tender.

4 Transfer roast and carrots to a plate, reserving drippings in Dutch oven. Cover roast and carrots loosely with aluminum foil, and keep warm. Skim fat from pan drippings; place Dutch oven over medium-high, and cook, stirring often, 12 minutes or until drippings are reduced by half (should equal about 3 cups). Whisk together flour and ½ cup water in a small bowl until smooth. Stir flour mixture into reduced drippings, and bring to a light boil, stirring often. Reduce heat to low, and simmer, stirring often, 5 minutes or until thickened. Stir in butter until melted; remove gravy from heat.

5 Cut roast across the grain into thin slices; cut carrots into desired-size pieces. Serve with gravy, and sprinkle with chopped parsley.

Daddy's Charcoal-Grilled Angus Rib-Eyes

The keys to this recipe are technique and simplicity—the charcoal flavors the tender meat. And because I season it at the last minute with salt, the meat remains juicy. I'm forever indebted to my father for teaching me the benefits of charcoal cooking, and like most of his teachings, it's a lesson in patience: a bit of extra time and effort (and no shortcuts) is always worth the greater result. Thanks, Big Rod!

HANDS-ON **10 MIN.** TOTAL **45 MIN.**
SERVES **4**

1 Let steak stand at room temperature 30 minutes. Meanwhile, preheat charcoal grill or smoker to 350°-400° (medium-high). (Coals will completely ash over.) Brush both sides of steaks with oil; sprinkle with pepper.

2 Grill steaks, covered with grill lid, 3 minutes. Rotate steaks 45 degrees, creating nice grill marks, and grill, covered with grill lid, 2 more minutes. Turn steaks over, and grill, covered with grill lid, 3 more minutes or until a meat thermometer inserted in thickest portion of steak reaches 135° (medium-rare). Transfer steaks to a cutting board, and cover loosely with aluminum foil. Let stand 5 minutes.

3 Sprinkle both sides of steaks with salt. Place steaks on serving plates, or cut diagonally across the grain into thin slices before serving.

⋛ INGREDIENTS ⋚

4 (12-oz.) rib-eye steaks
  (about 1¼-inch thick)
2 Tbsp. extra virgin olive oil
1 Tbsp. freshly ground black pepper
1 Tbsp. kosher salt

Old Smokey

Other than the times Mississippi State beats Ole Miss in football, I've never seen my father happier than when he found a brand-new Old Smokey grill—just like his old one—in a mom-and-pop hardware store during a family vacation in Florida. My dad, a former cattleman, was immediately taken back to his bachelor days living in an apartment complex in Valdosta, Georgia. Apparently, Dad was quite the grillmaster during those times, grilling steaks and pork chops on Old Smokey when the weekend finally arrived. Mama even recalls one of their first dates as being a home-cooked meal on this mystical device. Hey, I guess I get the "cooking for women" thing from somewhere!

Pan-Seared Venison Backstrap Medallions

I like to remove any silver skin, and slice the backstrap into medallions. You'll find that these cook up rather quickly in a cast-iron pan, leaving just a bit of drippings to create a rich sauce. The key to cooking venison—and most game— is to keep a watchful eye on the meat. Since it's so lean, it cooks faster than farm-raised beef or other animals. The savory sauce not only enhances the flavor, but also adds a bit of moisture to this outstanding piece of meat.

HANDS-ON 25 MIN. TOTAL 55 MIN.

SERVES 4

⇒ INGREDIENTS ⇐

1½ lb. venison backstrap,
    cut into 1½-inch medallions*
¼ cup extra virgin olive oil
2 Tbsp. balsamic vinegar
1 tsp. kosher salt, divided
¾ tsp. freshly ground black pepper
2 garlic cloves, crushed
2 Tbsp. minced shallot
2 Tbsp. unsalted butter, divided
½ cup dry red wine
1 cup beef stock
1 fresh rosemary sprig
Garnish: chopped fresh rosemary

*2 (14-oz.) packages Venison Medallions
from D'Artagnan may be substituted.
To order, visit www.dartagnan.com.

1 Combine medallions, oil, vinegar, ¾ tsp. salt, ½ tsp. pepper, and garlic in a large zip-top plastic freezer bag, turning to coat medallions. Let stand at room temperature 30 minutes.

2 Place a 12-inch cast-iron skillet over medium-high heat 1 minute or until hot. Remove medallions from marinade, shaking off any excess marinade; discard marinade. Place half of medallions into hot skillet, and cook 2 minutes on each side or until browned. Remove from heat, and transfer medallions to a plate, reserving drippings in skillet; cover medallions tightly with aluminum foil, and keep warm. Repeat with remaining medallions.

3 Return skillet with reserved drippings to medium-high heat; add shallot and 1 Tbsp. butter, and cook, stirring constantly, 1 minute or until shallot is golden. Add wine, and cook, stirring with a wooden spoon to loosen any browned bits from bottom of skillet, 1 minute. Cook, stirring occasionally, 2 more minutes or until wine is reduced by three-fourths and mixture is thick and syrupy. Add beef stock and rosemary sprig, and bring to a simmer; cook 6 minutes or until mixture is reduced by half.

4 Remove skillet from heat, and discard rosemary. Add remaining 1 Tbsp. butter, stirring until butter melts. Stir in remaining ¼ tsp. salt and ¼ tsp. pepper. Place medallions on plates, and drizzle with pan sauce; serve immediately.

THE MOST TENDER CUT

It's a rarity to get out of the hunting camp with the backstraps in tow. For those unfamiliar with the term, "backstrap" is the loin portion of a deer. It's arguably the most coveted and tender cut of meat, along with the actual tenderloin, because it's a muscle that the animal rarely uses. Unlike the other edible parts of the deer, the backstrap is also quite accessible when field dressing the animal—making an incision near the vertebrae from the hindquarter and down toward the neck of the animal. For that reason, many gentlemen harvest these delicious cuts to serve as a post-hunt celebratory meal.

TRIED +
TRUE SIDES

Oven "Fried" Okra

Okra is one of my all-time favorite ingredients, and it plays a vital role in many Southern and Creole dishes—mainly due to the fact that it can stand up on its own as well as act as a thickening agent in soups and stews. Many folks tend to associate Southern cuisine with exclusively fried dishes, but that sentiment couldn't be further from the truth. I relish the opportunity to recreate Southern fried classics by giving them modern-day twists that emphasize health and moderation.

Instead of battering the okra and deep-frying it in peanut oil, per the traditional method, I simply coat it in a bit of olive oil and season it lightly with salt and pepper. This allows the actual flavor of the okra to remain the star of the dish, which is always better in my opinion. For an indulgent twist, I like to top these little guys with a light layer of finely grated Parmigiano-Reggiano cheese right when they come out of the oven.

HANDS-ON **4 MIN.** TOTAL **29 MIN.**

SERVES **4**

⩴ INGREDIENTS ⩴

1 lb. fresh okra, trimmed

2 Tbsp. extra virgin olive oil

¼ tsp. kosher salt

¼ tsp. freshly ground black pepper

2 Tbsp. freshly grated Parmigiano-Reggiano cheese

1 Preheat oven to 400°. Toss okra with oil, salt, and pepper in a shallow pan until blended. Arrange okra in a single layer.

2 Bake at 400° for 25 minutes. Transfer okra to a bowl, add cheese, and toss until coated. Serve immediately.

Gent's Tips

I always try to buy okra pods that are bright green in color and smaller in size, about the size of your index finger. These younger, smaller pods are often more tender and less fibrous. Always be sure to wash the okra thoroughly in cold water prior to prepping.

Stewed Tomatoes + Okra

This hearty, vegan-friendly dish is one of my go-to sides, whether it is served alone or atop white rice to make a full meal. It is traditionally prepared in bacon drippings, but I prefer to stick to fresh tomatoes and okra. Following my method allows the starches in the okra to thicken the mixture, providing the ideal stewed consistency. If you only have frozen okra or canned tomatoes, don't fret—just use the same amounts listed below. For the tomatoes, substitute the juices for the wine or vegetable stock.

At dinner parties, guests always ask me why my Stewed Tomatoes and Okra dish is so much better than the version they grew up eating. Well, I suppose now's as good a time as any to come clean. My secret ingredient is a hint of curry powder toasted with the onions and oil to add a fragrant, depth of flavor.

HANDS-ON 45 MIN. TOTAL **45 MIN.**

SERVES **4**

1 Place a 12-inch cast-iron skillet over medium heat 1 minute or until hot; add oil. Add onion, and sauté 5 minutes or just until tender. Add garlic and next 3 ingredients; sauté 3-4 minutes or until garlic is fragrant and just turns golden.

2 Add tomatoes, sauté 3 minutes or until tomatoes begin to release juices. Add wine, and cook, stirring with a wooden spoon to loosen any browned bits from bottom of skillet, 1 minute. Add okra, reduce heat to medium-low, and simmer partially covered and stirring occasionally, 25 minutes or until okra is tender. Stir in desired amount of hot sauce, and serve immediately.

⇒ INGREDIENTS ⇐

1 Tbsp. extra virgin olive oil
1 medium Vidalia or sweet onion, diced
2 garlic cloves, minced
1 tsp. kosher salt
½ tsp. freshly ground black pepper
¼ tsp. curry powder
3 cups coarsely chopped tomatoes
¾ cup dry white wine*
1 lb. fresh okra, trimmed and cut into
  ½-inch pieces (2 cups)
Hot sauce

*Vegetable stock may be substituted.

Pimiento Mac 'n' Cheese

Folks who are not from the South tend to balk at the fact that mac 'n' cheese is listed at as a "vegetable side dish" on the menus of many establishments. But you won't hear me complaining about the misnomer. I love tacking on a little mac 'n' cheese to help round out my meal at my local meat and three.

My Nashville friends have been begging me for this recipe for years, so I figure I may as well come clean and disclose all my secrets! When making this dish at home, I like to put a twist on this classic by combining the rich, creamy mac 'n' cheese flavor with another traditional Southern favorite—pimiento cheese. Instead of mayonnaise, I use a little bit of Greek yogurt to provide even more richness, healthy protein, and tangy flavor that is simply irresistible. This pairs well with any meat, and it also stands up as a hearty side on a "vegetable plate."

HANDS-ON 31 MIN.   TOTAL 1 HR., 16 MIN.

SERVES 8

⋛ INGREDIENTS ⋚

2 tsp. kosher salt, divided
1 (16-oz.) package cavatappi pasta
4 Tbsp. unsalted butter
4 Tbsp. all-purpose flour
3 cups milk
½ tsp. dry mustard
Pinch of ground nutmeg
Dash of hot sauce
6 cups (24 oz.) shredded extra-sharp
   Cheddar cheese, divided
1 cup plain Greek yogurt
1 (4-oz.) jar diced pimiento, drained
Vegetable cooking spray

1 Bring 2 qt. water to a boil in a Dutch oven over high heat. Stir in 1 tsp. salt; add pasta, and cook 8 minutes or until almost al dente.

2 Preheat oven to 350°. Melt butter in a medium saucepan over medium heat; whisk in flour until smooth. Cook, whisking constantly, 1 minute. Gradually whisk in milk, next 3 ingredients, and remaining 1 tsp. salt. Bring milk mixture to a light boil, whisking frequently; be careful not to scorch milk. Cook, whisking occasionally, 5 minutes or until thickened. Remove from heat, and stir in 4 cups cheese until melted and smooth. Keep warm.

3 Stir together yogurt, pimiento, and remaining 2 cups cheese in a small bowl until blended.

4 Lightly grease a 13- x 9-inch baking dish with cooking spray. Combine pasta, cheese sauce, and yogurt mixture in prepared baking dish, stirring until blended. Bake at 350° for 35 minutes or until bubbly and golden brown. Let stand 10 minutes before serving.

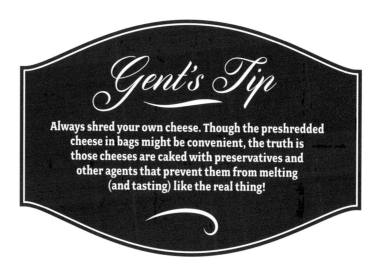

Gent's Tip

Always shred your own cheese. Though the preshredded cheese in bags might be convenient, the truth is those cheeses are caked with preservatives and other agents that prevent them from melting (and tasting) like the real thing!

Baked Cheese Grits

Mama used to make grits every morning before I headed off to school, claiming that they'd "stick to my ribs" throughout the long day ahead. She was right. A bowl of grits is both comforting and delicious.

For this recipe, I like to use quick-cooking grits on the stove. From there, I mix in some love and bake everything off so that you can serve this side in nice, uniform portions—it will cut nicely into squares. This dish goes great as a side to meat or fish, as well as grilled portobello mushrooms, for a hearty and satisfying vegetarian-friendly meal.

HANDS-ON 10 MIN. TOTAL **47 MIN.**

SERVES **6**

1 Preheat oven to 375°. Melt butter in a medium saucepan over medium-high heat. Add grits, and cook, stirring constantly with a wooden spoon, 1 minute or until grits are coated and toasted. Stir in salt and garlic powder. Whisk in 6 cups water, making sure no lumps form. Bring mixture to a boil, stirring frequently. Cover, reduce heat to low, and simmer, stirring occasionally, 7-8 minutes or until grits are tender and creamy. Add 1 cup cheese and tomatoes and chiles, stirring until blended. Remove from heat.

2 Lightly grease a 13- x- 9-inch baking dish with cooking spray. Spoon grits mixture into prepared baking dish; sprinkle with remaining 1 cup cheese. Bake at 375° for 30 minutes. Remove from oven, and let stand 10 minutes before serving.

⇒ INGREDIENTS ⇐

- 1 Tbsp. unsalted butter
- 2 cups uncooked quick-cooking grits
- 1½ tsp. kosher salt
- ½ tsp. garlic powder
- 2 cups (8 oz.) shredded extra-sharp Cheddar cheese, divided
- 1 (10-oz.) can diced tomatoes and green chiles, undrained
- Vegetable cooking spray
- Garnish: sliced green onions

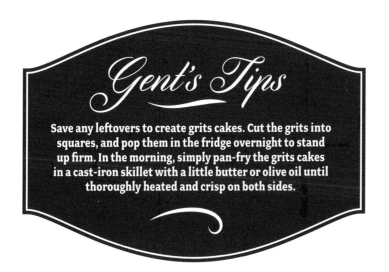

Gent's Tips

Save any leftovers to create grits cakes. Cut the grits into squares, and pop them in the fridge overnight to stand up firm. In the morning, simply pan-fry the grits cakes in a cast-iron skillet with a little butter or olive oil until thoroughly heated and crisp on both sides.

Collard Greens + Pepper Sauce + Potlikker

When I was a kid, Mama used to make a big ole pot of greens during the afternoon for supper that evening. I loved to douse my greens with pepper sauce, which I'd shake on everything from greens to black-eyed peas and barbecue. I also like sopping up the potlikker with hot cornbread or muffins. You can substitute mustard or turnip greens or even kale for the collard greens. When time permits, it's best to make the pepper sauce several days or weeks in advance to give the peppers time to flavor the vinegar.

HANDS-ON 31 MIN. TOTAL **2 HR., 39 MIN.**
SERVES 8

≷ INGREDIENTS ≷

4 garlic cloves
6 hickory-smoked bacon slices, coarsely chopped
1 medium Vidalia or sweet onion, coarsely chopped
1 qt. chicken stock or reduced-sodium chicken broth
1 Tbsp. apple cider vinegar
3 lb. fresh collard greens, washed, trimmed, and coarsely chopped
1 tsp. kosher salt
Pepper Sauce

1 Smash garlic using flat side of a knife. Place a large Dutch oven over medium-high heat 1 minute or until hot; add bacon, and cook, stirring occasionally, 6 minutes or until crisp. Add onion and smashed garlic, and sauté 5 minutes or just until tender.

2 Add stock and vinegar, and bring to a light boil. Stir in greens, and return to a simmer. Cover, reduce heat to medium-low, and simmer, stirring occasionally, 2 hours or until greens are tender and fully cooked. Stir in salt. Serve with Pepper Sauce.

Pepper Sauce

HANDS-ON 8 MIN. TOTAL **2 HR., 8 MIN.,** PLUS 1 DAY FOR CHILLING
MAKES 3 PINTS

≷ INGREDIENTS ≷

2½ cups white vinegar
2 Tbsp. sugar
½ tsp. kosher salt
20 assorted fresh peppers, such as serrano and jalapeño peppers

1 Bring vinegar, sugar, and salt to a boil in a small saucepan over medium-high heat. Meanwhile, pack peppers tightly into 3 clean, sterilized pint-size glass canning jars. Pour enough hot vinegar mixture over peppers to cover completely, filling to 1 inch from top. Cover at once with metal lids, and screw on bands. Cool to room temperature (about 2 hours). Chill at least 24 hours before serving; refrigerate up to 2 weeks.

MARY MAC'S

An elderly cook at Mary Mac's Tea Room, a local Atlanta establishment known for curating and preserving some of the South's most popular dishes, told me the secret for making perfect collard greens. Though most folks simply cook their greens in water, the chefs at Mary Mac's cook theirs in chicken stock, resulting in some of the most flavorful greens I've ever tasted. Not to mention the fact that the potlikker—the leftover stock (juice) from the greens, which is loaded with vitamins—is even more superb.

Grilled Corn + Tequila-Lime Butter

I serve fresh, grilled corn at all of my summertime cookouts. This quick dish simply goes on the grill—easy as that. I like to keep the husks on so that the corn is nice and juicy and you get smoky, grilled flavors in each bite. Grilling with the husks on also makes for a rustic, authentic presentation.

This recipe is best made on a charcoal grill—but you can still get the same effect on a gas grill. When you are at the market, select fresh, good-quality corn. I peel back the husk at the top of each ear to reveal the kernels, which should be tightly packed and plump—if they look dry, move on to the next ear.

I up the ante with my Tequila-Lime Butter, which I spread over the hot corn right when it comes off the grill. This butter has the kick of tequila, along with spicy heat from jalapeño pepper, all mellowed out a bit with fresh lime juice and the natural creaminess of butter.

HANDS-ON 27 MIN. **TOTAL 37 MIN.**
SERVES 8

1 Prepare Corn: Preheat grill to 300°-350° (medium). Pull husks down, keeping husks attached and intact; remove and discard silks. Pull husks back up to cover corn. Place corn in salted water to cover in a large bowl or stockpot, and let stand 10 minutes.

2 Meanwhile, prepare Tequila-Lime Butter: Combine butter and next 5 ingredients in a small bowl, stirring with a wooden spoon until blended. Spoon butter mixture onto plastic wrap; roll tightly, forming a log. Chill until ready to use.

3 Remove corn from water. Place corn in husks on cooking grate, and grill, covered with grill lid, 15-20 minutes or until husks are blackened, turning every 5 minutes. Place corn on a serving plate, and fold back or remove husks.

4 Cut butter mixture into 8 pieces. Spread 1 piece of butter mixture on each cob until melted, turning to coat each cob completely. Serve immediately.

CORN
8 ears fresh corn with husks
1 tsp. kosher salt

TEQUILA-LIME BUTTER
½ cup unsalted butter, softened
1 tsp. seeded, finely diced
   jalapeño pepper
1 tsp. lime zest
1½ tsp. fresh lime juice
1 tsp. tequila
½ tsp. kosher salt

Fresh-Picked Creamed Corn

During the summer, Daddy often returned from a long day on the farm with a bit of a bonus paid out in either fresh greens or corn. My sister, Ashley, and I were required to take a break from our fun—playing Two Square while listening to the latest Guns N' Roses album —to either shuck corn or wash greens. Mama and Daddy were so not hip to the tunes of the late 80s—at least that's what we thought, so Ashley and I would sit in our garage and "labor" away for a few hours so that Mama could get to work in the kitchen.

Creamed corn is a staple throughout the South—often a harvest time side, when there's corn aplenty. I like to put a Mediterranean-inspired play on it by using garlic, fresh basil, and indulgent Parmigiano-Reggiano cheese.

HANDS-ON **40 MIN.** TOTAL **40 MIN.**

SERVES **6**

INGREDIENTS

8 ears fresh corn, husks removed

2 Tbsp. olive oil

1 medium Vidalia or sweet onion, finely minced

1 jalapeño pepper, seeded and finely diced

3 garlic cloves, finely minced

1 tsp. kosher salt

½ tsp. freshly ground black pepper

½ cup dry white wine

½ cup freshly grated Parmigiano-Reggiano cheese

1 cup heavy cream

1 tsp. finely chopped fresh basil

1 Hold each cob upright on a cutting board, and carefully cut downward, cutting corn kernels from cobs into a large bowl to equal 5 cups. Scrape corn milk and any remaining pulp from cobs into a separate bowl (amount of milk will vary depending on freshness of corn). Discard cobs.

2 Place a large stainless steel skillet over medium heat 1 minute or until hot; add oil. Add onion and jalapeño pepper, and sauté 8 minutes or until onion is translucent and tender. Add garlic and corn kernels; sprinkle with salt and pepper, and sauté 10 minutes. Add wine, and cook, stirring with a wooden spoon to loosen any browned bits from bottom of skillet, 2 minutes. Add corn milk and pulp, and cook, stirring often, 2-3 minutes.

3 Stir in Parmigiano-Reggiano cheese, and enough heavy cream to reach desired consistency; remove skillet from heat. Process mixture with a handheld (immersion) blender until smooth and creamy, leaving some corn kernels whole. Stir in chopped basil until blended; serve immediately.

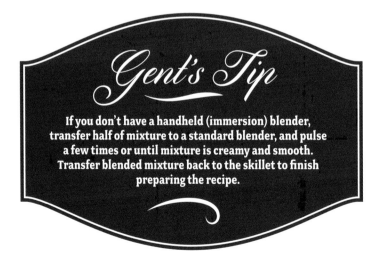

Gent's Tip

If you don't have a handheld (immersion) blender, transfer half of mixture to a standard blender, and pulse a few times or until mixture is creamy and smooth. Transfer blended mixture back to the skillet to finish preparing the recipe.

Sautéed Squash + Vidalia Onions + Chèvre

Throughout the South, folks are accustomed to eating squash-and-cheese casserole as a side dish, something that is just as common as mac 'n' cheese. Usually overloaded with processed can soups and fillers, it seems to do squash, one of my favorite vegetables, a bit of an injustice. So instead, I change things up entirely, which as you may have picked up on, is just what I do. I coax out the same nutty flavors of the squash by sautéing it with a mix of sweet and savory onions. To top everything off, I add creamy, tangy goat cheese, which develops into a sauce that surrounds the tender squash, and finishes with the sweet flavor of fresh basil. This is your modern take on squash-and-cheese casserole—trust me, it tastes just as good and refreshing as your grandma's, without the guilt and gut.

HANDS-ON 20 MIN. TOTAL 20 MIN.

SERVES 4

1 Place a large skillet over medium heat 1 minute or until hot; add oil. Add onion, salt, pepper, and garlic; sauté 6 minutes or until tender and translucent. Add squash, and sauté 4-6 minutes or just until tender.

2 Add goat cheese, and cook, stirring constantly, 2 minutes or until cheese melts and is smooth. Sprinkle with basil, and toss until blended. Serve immediately.

⇒ INGREDIENTS ⇐

2 Tbsp. extra virgin olive oil

1 large Vidalia or sweet onion, roughly chopped

1 tsp. kosher salt

½ tsp. freshly ground black pepper

1 garlic clove, minced

3 yellow squash, cut diagonally into ½-inch slices

4 oz. goat cheese log, cut into pieces

2 tsp. finely chopped fresh basil

NOBLE SPRINGS DAIRY

Just a quick 30-minute drive from my home in Nashville sits Noble Springs Dairy in Franklin, Tenn. Husband and wife Dustin and Justyne Noble are not only some of the finest people I've ever met, but they are also passionate about their beautiful farm and their animals. Luckily for the rest of us that passion also translates to incredible goat milk, yogurt, and cheese (see page 278). Young farmers like the Nobles are carrying on a proud southern tradition of farming and food.

Chorizo Roasted Potatoes + Vidalia Onions

This is one of my effortless side dishes for ramping up color and flavor, not to mention adding in a nice kick of spicy, smoky goodness. Fresh chorizo sausages can be found in the meat section of almost any major supermarket.

I like to "fry" up the potatoes in the chorizo drippings prior to baking them in the oven. Served for breakfast alongside a plate of scrambled eggs or as a side dish at supper, this decadently simple recipe aims to please.

HANDS-ON 20 MIN. TOTAL 20 MIN.

SERVES 10-12

⇒ INGREDIENTS ⇐

½ lb. fresh chorizo sausage, casings removed

1 large Vidalia or sweet onion, cut into wedges

3 lb. small Yukon gold potatoes, quartered

3 garlic cloves, minced

1 tsp. kosher salt

1 tsp. freshly ground black pepper

Garnish: chopped fresh cilantro, sliced green onion tops, or chopped fresh flat-leaf parsley

1 Preheat oven to 425°. Place a 12-inch cast-iron skillet over medium-high heat 1 minute or until hot. Add sausage, and cook, breaking sausage into large pieces, 4 minutes or until meat is no longer pink. Transfer sausage to a plate using a slotted spoon, reserving drippings in skillet.

2 Add half of onion wedges and potatoes to hot drippings in skillet, being careful not to overcrowd; cook 2-3 minutes on each side or until browned. Transfer browned onion and potatoes to a plate, reserving drippings in skillet. Repeat procedure with remaining onion wedges and potatoes. Return all onion wedges and potatoes to skillet, and stir in garlic, salt, and pepper.

3 Transfer skillet to oven, and bake at 425°, stirring occasionally, for 30 minutes or until potatoes are golden brown and fork-tender. Remove skillet from oven; stir in cooked chorizo, and serve immediately.

MY PAPA LAMAR

I've been very blessed to spend quality time with both sets of grandparents throughout much of my adult life. There's so much to learn from their generation—most commonly referred to as the Greatest Generation—as their values of service and patriotic ideals have been a transformative part of my life. My Papa, on Daddy's side, is my last remaining grandparent, and he's a true Southern gentleman.

Papa was born and raised in the small town of Enterprise, Miss., just outside Meridian, for those who've passed through on Interstate 20. Other than a brief stint in Salzburg, Austria, in '45 to join the liberation in Europe, Papa has made this small town the center of his world for almost 90 years. Actually, I should say the center of his world is his angel, Dorothy, for whom he was devoted to in life and marriage for over 67 years.

Upon returning from the war, Papa delivered mail for the USPS to residents in Enterprise and surrounding towns, while maintaining a herd of cattle and timberland on the family farm. He raised my father and two daughters (Aunt Beth and Aunt Lynne) on the lessons of hard work and finding the joy in life through loving his ultimate father, Jesus Christ. A master Mason for over 60 years, and a church usher at Enterprise United Methodist Church, where he's attended services his entire lifetime, Papa embodies the value of self-sacrifice and service to others more than any man I've ever met.

For decades, Papa maintained a robust garden in his backyard of peppers, corn, tomatoes, pole beans, butter beans, and the occasional watermelon or two. It was always this garden and his livestock, that allowed Papa to ensure that the family was well-fed. Though his eyesight is no longer what it used to be, Papa still has a crop or two growing in his backyard garden—and trust me, he knows how to fire up that ole Massey Ferguson tractor when harvest comes around!

Better Butter Beans

As kids, we visited our grandparents throughout our childhood. I can remember my sister Ashley and me sitting on the back screen porch on many sweltering summer evenings, hulling fresh butter beans to a chorus of humming cicadas and chirping crickets in the backyard pasture. Butter beans were always my favorite vegetable on the dinner table mainly because I liked their name. Truth be told, butter beans are the same as Lima beans, so it's fair to say that most kids probably don't share my sentiment. That's until you cook these guys the way I make 'em. Prepared simply, and with a little love, let me show you how to make Better Butter Beans. This one's for you, Papa—all my love.

HANDS-ON 10 MIN. TOTAL **50 MIN.**

SERVES **6**

1 Rinse and sort through beans for any that are chipped or shriveled. Place a medium saucepan over medium-high heat 1 minute or until hot. Add beans and stock, and bring to a boil. Cover, reduce heat to medium-low, and simmer 35 minutes or just until beans are tender. Drain beans.

2 Meanwhile, place a 12-inch cast-iron skillet over medium heat 1 minute or until hot; add butter. Sauté shallot in melted butter 2 minutes. Add bacon, and cook, stirring occasionally, 5 minutes or until bacon is crisp and shallots are tender. Add beans, and season with salt and pepper; cook, stirring occasionally, 3 minutes or until thoroughly heated. Serve immediately.

⇒ INGREDIENTS ⇐

4 cups shelled fresh butter beans
  (about 1 lb.)
6 cups chicken stock or broth*
2 Tbsp. unsalted butter
1 shallot, finely diced
2 hickory-smoked bacon slices, diced
¼ tsp. kosher salt
¼ tsp. freshly ground black pepper

*6 cups water and 1 tsp. salt may be substituted.

Kitchen Sink Baked Beans

Sometimes my greatest recipes are the result of necessity. In Georgia, we are not known to get many snowstorms—and when we do...Lord watch out. There's a run on white bread, eggs, and cold beer at the grocery store to the likes you've never seen. Just getting to the store is almost impossible. We love our 4 x 4s, but I'll be darned if I've ever seen a Southerner drive properly in the snow, me included.

Several years back, I was snowed in in Athens, Georgia. When it came time to make a meal, I had to literally pull out everything I had in the cupboards and fridge to make something hearty enough to stand up to the cold outside. I threw in the whole kitchen sink but fortunately, I turned out a meal that is now a favorite side dish at all summer cookouts and dinner parties.

HANDS-ON 12 MIN. TOTAL **1 HR., 10 MIN.**

SERVES **6-8**

≥ INGREDIENTS ≤

1 Tbsp. extra virgin olive oil

½ medium Vidalia or sweet onion, finely diced

½ green bell pepper, finely diced

2 garlic cloves, minced

½ tsp. kosher salt

1 (15-oz.) can black beans, drained and rinsed

1 (15.8-oz.) can great Northern beans, drained and rinsed

1 (16-oz.) can dark kidney beans, drained and rinsed

⅓ cup ketchup

¼ cup bottled vinegar-based barbecue sauce

¼ cup dark brown sugar

¼ cup light molasses

1 Tbsp. Worcestershire sauce

1½ tsp. yellow mustard

4 hickory-smoked bacon slices

1 Preheat oven to 350°. Place a 12-inch cast-iron skillet over medium heat 1 minute or until hot; add oil. Stir in onion and next 3 ingredients; sauté 7 minutes or just until onion is tender and translucent.

2 Stir in black beans and next 8 ingredients. Top with bacon slices. Transfer skillet to oven, and bake at 350° for 30 minutes.

3 Increase oven temperature to 450°, and bake for 18 minutes or until bacon is crisp. Remove from oven, and let stand 10 minutes before serving.

JD's Whiskey-Glazed Carrots

My philosophy is that life—as well as cooking—is always better when a bit of whiskey is involved. Fortunately, one of Tennessee's finest and most famous distilleries, Jack Daniel's, is located in Lynchburg, Tennessee—just a short drive from my home in Nashville. Such proximity ensures that I'm never out of stock on this fine drink. Needless to say, we are mighty blessed here in Tennessee!

I like adding a shot or so of this spirit to this recipe as the rich flavors of the reduced whiskey play nicely off the sweet, caramelized flavor of the carrots. Oftentimes, I leave the bottle of whiskey out on the counter to let my guests know that I mean serious business—I find that folks always get excited when a bit of alcohol is used as an ingredient in their meal. Of course, feel free to substitute any of your favorite bourbon or whiskey you have on hand. This side is delicious and also quick and easy to prepare.

HANDS-ON 28 MIN. TOTAL **28 MIN.**

SERVES **4**

1 Place a 12-inch cast-iron skillet over medium-high heat 1 minute or until hot. Melt ¼ cup butter in hot skillet; add half of carrots, and sauté 3 minutes or just until lightly browned. Transfer carrots to a plate using a slotted spoon. Repeat with remaining carrots.

2 Remove skillet from heat, step away, and add whiskey. If desired, carefully light whiskey with a long match or long multipurpose lighter; let flames die down. Carefully return skillet to medium-high heat. Add brown sugar, orange juice, and remaining ¼ cup butter; cook, stirring frequently, 2 minutes or until butter melts and sugar dissolves. Return carrots to skillet; stir in salt and pepper. Cover, reduce heat to medium-low, and cook, stirring occasionally, 10 minutes or until tender.

3 Remove skillet from heat, and transfer carrots to a serving platter with a slotted spoon. Pour pan juices over carrots. Serve immediately.

⇒ INGREDIENTS ⇐

½ cup unsalted butter, divided

10 large carrots, peeled and cut into ½-inch slices (5 cups)

½ cup Jack Daniel's whiskey

¼ cup firmly packed light brown sugar

2 Tbsp. fresh orange juice

½ tsp. kosher salt

½ tsp. freshly ground black pepper

Garnish: finely chopped chives

Guiltless Cauliflower Puree

This is a staple recipe around my house, especially when Callie and I are craving a comforting side without the guilt. Trust me, the next time you are thinking about making carb-laden, buttery mashed potatoes, follow this recipe—you won't be disappointed.

I like to substitute Greek yogurt and olive oil for the milk and butter to give this side dish an added dose of protein and good fats and create a rich, velvety texture. Lower in fat and carbs, while also packing in some protein, this dish is also pretty budget-friendly. I use frozen cauliflower florets, which are not only cheaper and less of a mess than a whole head, but it's also something I can find year-round when our mashed potato craving sets in! The key to this dish is using a handheld (immersion) blender to puree the cauliflower until it is light and smooth, working a bit of air into the mixture. See "Gent's Tip" on page 219 for an alternate blending method.

HANDS-ON **6 MIN.** TOTAL **15 MIN.**

SERVES **6**

⋛ INGREDIENTS ⋚

2 (16-oz.) packages frozen
  cauliflower florets
2 Tbsp. extra virgin olive oil
1½ tsp. kosher salt
½ tsp. freshly ground black pepper
½ tsp. garlic powder
¼ cup plain Greek yogurt
¼ cup (1 oz.) freshly grated Parmigiano-
  Reggiano cheese
Kosher salt
Freshly ground black pepper

1 Bring 1 cup water to a boil in a medium saucepan over medium-high heat. Arrange cauliflower in a steamer basket over boiling water; cover and steam 10 minutes or until cauliflower is tender. Drain cauliflower, reserving cooking liquid. Return cauliflower to pan, and cook 1 minute or until excess water evaporates.

2 Remove pan from heat; add oil and next 5 ingredients. Process mixture with a handheld (immersion) blender 1½ minutes or until light and smooth. If you want a thinner consistency, add reserved cooking liquid, 1 Tbsp. at a time, until puree reaches desired consistency. Season with additional salt and pepper to taste. Serve immediately.

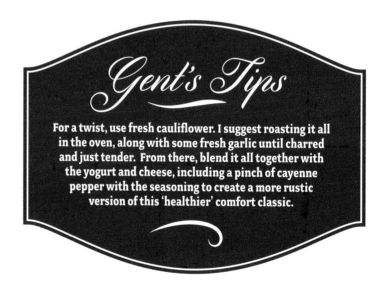

Gent's Tips

For a twist, use fresh cauliflower. I suggest roasting it all in the oven, along with some fresh garlic until charred and just tender. From there, blend it all together with the yogurt and cheese, including a pinch of cayenne pepper with the seasoning to create a more rustic version of this 'healthier' comfort classic.

R.G.B. Slaw

No Southern cookout is complete without a side of slaw. Served on its own or on top of a barbecue sandwich, there's no doubt that slaw is a favorite dish or condiment of our culture. This recipe makes use of red cabbage, green chives, and blue cheese—hence the "RGB" moniker. I've lightened up the traditional coleslaw by substituting vinaigrette for the mayonnaise. The light acidity from the vinegar and tangy blue cheese create a flavor combination that's out of this world. For an extra kick of heat, toss in some very thinly sliced fresh jalapeño pepper.

HANDS-ON 5 MIN. TOTAL **15 MIN.**
MAKES **11 CUPS**

1 Combine all ingredients in a serving bowl, and toss until thoroughly coated. Let stand 10 minutes before serving. If not serving immediately, cover and chill up to 1 hour.

INGREDIENTS

1 head red cabbage (about 2 lb.), finely shredded
1 bunch fresh chives, cut diagonally into 1-inch pieces
8 oz. crumbled blue cheese
⅓ cup extra virgin olive oil
3 Tbsp. red wine vinegar
1½ tsp. kosher salt
1 tsp. freshly ground black pepper
1 jalapeño pepper, very thinly sliced

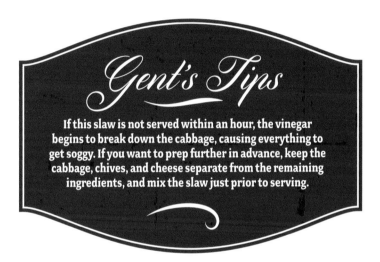

Gent's Tips

If this slaw is not served within an hour, the vinegar begins to break down the cabbage, causing everything to get soggy. If you want to prep further in advance, keep the cabbage, chives, and cheese separate from the remaining ingredients, and mix the slaw just prior to serving.

Maque Choux

Comforting, a bit spicy and sweet, creamy, and utterly delicious—that's pretty much the perfect description for this Louisiana favorite. Traditionalists might use bacon fat or even sausage as the base of this dish, but I prefer to keep it entirely focused on just vegetables. By charring the corn in the cast-iron skillet before you remove it from the cob, you really start to develop some rich, nutty flavors. This dish pairs well with any grilled fish or meat.

HANDS-ON 29 MIN. TOTAL 29 MIN.

SERVES 4

⇒ INGREDIENTS ⇐

3 ears fresh corn, husks removed

2 Tbsp. extra virgin olive oil

1 medium Vidalia or sweet onion, finely diced

1 green bell pepper, finely diced

½ tsp. freshly ground black pepper

¼ tsp. ground red pepper

2½ tsp. kosher salt, divided

2 garlic cloves, minced

1 (14.5-oz.) can diced tomatoes, undrained

½ cup heavy cream

Freshly ground black pepper

Garnish: thinly sliced green onions

1 Place a 12-inch cast-iron skillet over medium-high heat 1 minute or until hot. Add corn, and cook, turning occasionally, 3-5 minutes or until kernels are slightly charred; remove skillet from heat. Hold each cob upright on a cutting board, and carefully cut downward, cutting kernels from cobs; reserve corn milk and pulp. Discard cobs.

2 Return skillet to medium-high heat, and add oil, next 4 ingredients, and 1 tsp. salt. Sauté 10 minutes or until onions are translucent and tender. Add garlic, and sauté 2 minutes.

3 Add tomatoes, and cook, stirring to loosen any browned bits from bottom of skillet, 1 minute. Return corn and reserved corn milk and pulp to skillet, and bring to a light boil. Reduce heat to low, and simmer 5 minutes. Stir in cream, and simmer 2 minutes or until slightly thickened; remove skillet from heat. Season with remaining 1½ tsp. salt and additional freshly ground black pepper to taste. Serve immediately.

Sweet Peas + Bacon + Mascarpone

As a kid, I remember the few times Mama went out of town on a "girls trip" with Ms. Jamie and Ms. Emily, aka my "other" moms. Before leaving, Mama would whip up a casserole or two. Without fail, once those casseroles were devoured, we'd get in Dad's truck and head off to the grocery store to stock up on provisions—usually a box of brownies, ice cream, bread, eggs, milk, and a few cans of Le Sueur sweet peas. The Le Sueur peas were the side dish for Dad's grilled chicken.

The memories of those peas as a comforting side still remain strong—I've just grown up a bit. To keep things simple, I go with frozen peas instead of the soggier version that comes from the can. I enrich the experience with creamy mascarpone cheese, while topping it all off with crispy, crunchy bacon. Trust me—even Dad will readily admit that these are better.

HANDS-ON **18 MIN.** TOTAL **18 MIN.**

SERVES **4**

1 Place a skillet over medium heat 2 minutes or until hot. Add bacon, and cook, stirring occasionally, 4 minutes or until crisp. Remove bacon with a slotted spoon; drain bacon on paper towels, reserving drippings in skillet.

2 Sauté shallot in hot drippings 4 minutes or until tender. Add wine, and cook, stirring to loosen any browned bits from bottom of skillet, 30 seconds. Stir in peas, salt, and pepper, and cook 5 minutes or until peas are bright green and tender.

3 Fold in mascarpone cheese, and cook 1 minute or until cheese melts and mixture is creamy. Transfer to a serving dish, and sprinkle with bacon. Serve immediately.

⇒ INGREDIENTS ⇐

4 hickory-smoked bacon slices, diced
1 shallot, minced
¼ cup dry white wine*
1 (16-oz.) package frozen sweet peas, thawed
½ tsp. kosher salt
½ tsp. freshly ground black pepper
2 Tbsp. mascarpone cheese

*Reduced-sodium chicken broth may be substituted.

Gent's Tips

If you have fresh green peas, by all means use them! Just blanch them in some hot boiling water for a minute or so, and run them under cold water until completely cooled, and then follow the recipe above.

Roasted Brussels Sprouts + Pancetta

These days, it seems that Brussels sprouts are all the rage—and for good reason. These tasty gems are not the variety once served to you at your grandma's house. Instead, chefs around the country are making use of this healthy ingredient while transforming it into one of America's favorite side dishes.

Instead of bacon, I go with a few slices of pancetta. The reason I chose pancetta over bacon is because it's traditionally found at the deli counter, whereas bacon is typically sold in whole packs. This allows me to buy just what I need, instead of buying a whole package of bacon, which I may or may not use—let's get real, I'll probably use it. Regardless, I like the flexibility of being able to buy just what I need for each meal to keep costs down without sacrificing flavor.

HANDS-ON 5 MIN. **TOTAL 35 MIN.**

SERVES 4

≳ INGREDIENTS ≲

5 cups trimmed and halved Brussels
 sprouts (about 1½ lb.)
2 Tbsp. extra virgin olive oil
½ tsp. kosher salt
½ tsp. freshly ground black pepper
1 Tbsp. fresh lemon juice
1 (¼-inch-thick) pancetta slice, finely
 chopped (¼ cup)

1 Preheat oven to 375°. Place Brussels sprouts in a shallow pan, and drizzle with olive oil; sprinkle with salt and pepper. Add lemon juice and pancetta, and toss to coat.

2 Bake at 375° for 25-30 minutes or until Brussels sprouts are slightly browned and tender, stirring halfway through. Serve immediately.

Sweet Potato Smash

This dish is a great alternative to classic mashed potatoes. Compared to white potatoes, the sweet potato variety is loaded with vitamins A and C. It also boasts fewer calories, more fiber, and fewer carbs than most white potato varieties.

That being said, I do like to add a bit of love to this side with some butter and brown sugar. I save time by hand-mashing the potatoes—leaving the rustic, chunky texture. It's my way of letting guests know that this dish was made from scratch, and it's not out of a can or box. Of course, if you prefer a more consistent texture, you can always run the cooked potatoes through a potato ricer, blender, or food mill. This dish pairs well with most fish and meats, but it really shines with grilled pork chops and pork tenderloin.

HANDS-ON **20 MIN.** TOTAL **1 HR.**

SERVES **8**

1 Bring 3 qt. water to a boil in a large saucepan over high heat. Add potatoes, return to a boil, and cook 10 minutes or until fork-tender. Drain, and let rest uncovered to prevent them from becoming watery.

2 Add butter to pan, and melt over low heat; remove from heat. Return potatoes to pan, and add brown sugar and remaining ingredients. Mash with a potato masher until smooth and blended. Serve immediately.

⇒ INGREDIENTS ⇐

3 lb. sweet potatoes, peeled and cut into 1½-inch cubes

¼ cup butter

⅓ cup firmly packed light brown sugar

1 tsp. kosher salt

½ tsp. ground cinnamon

½ cup heavy cream

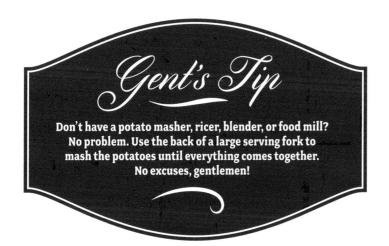

Gent's Tip

Don't have a potato masher, ricer, blender, or food mill? No problem. Use the back of a large serving fork to mash the potatoes until everything comes together. No excuses, gentlemen!

Nashville Farmers' Market Succotash

One of the best ways to celebrate the bounty of fresh ingredients is with a traditional succotash. Primarily corn and lima beans (butter beans), succotash is one of those dishes that can take on many forms based on what's fresh.

Mine varies according to what I can find locally. It's no coincidence that eating this dish reminds me of the good folks and friends at the Nashville Farmers' Market who have a hand in growing its fine ingredients.

HANDS-ON **48 MIN.** TOTAL **48 MIN.**

SERVES **6**

➤ INGREDIENTS ➤

4 ears fresh corn, husks removed
2 Tbsp. unsalted butter
2 Tbsp. extra virgin olive oil
1 Vidalia or sweet onion, finely chopped
1 red bell pepper, finely chopped
1 Tbsp. kosher salt
2½ tsp. freshly ground black pepper
3 garlic cloves, minced
2 cups fresh lima beans*
3 cups chopped tomatoes
½ lb. fresh okra, cut into 1-inch pieces
1 cup dry white wine**

*Frozen lima beans, thawed, may be substituted.

**Reduced-sodium chicken broth may be substituted.

1 Hold each cob upright on a cutting board, and carefully cut downward, cutting corn kernels from cobs into a large bowl to equal 2¼ cups. Discard cobs.

2 Place a 12-inch skillet over medium-high heat 1 minute or until hot; melt butter with olive oil in hot skillet. Add onion and next 3 ingredients, and sauté 8 minutes or until onion is tender and translucent. Add garlic, and sauté 1 minute or until fragrant.

3 Stir in corn kernels, lima beans, and next 2 ingredients. Add wine, and cook, stirring to loosen any browned bits from bottom of skillet, 1 minute. Reduce heat to medium-low, and simmer, partially covered and stirring occasionally, 25 minutes or until lima beans and okra are tender. Serve immediately.

THE NASHVILLE FARMERS' MARKET

On Saturday mornings I love to hop on my bike and ride downtown to the Nashville Farmers' Market, which has been in existence since the 1800s (and at its current location since the 1950s). Even the great flood of 2010 couldn't stop local farmers, artisans, and specialty purveyors from making it to market. I like to walk through the sheds filled with produce, picking up any and all that looks good. Admittedly, such a heavy load can make for a long bike ride home!

Cast-Iron Skillet Jalapeño Cornbread

No two things define Southern cooking better than cast iron and cornbread. Cornbread is the perfect complement to sop up hearty stews, or served on its own as a supplementary starch. Though you'll find many variations of this dish, the jalapeño variety tends to be my preference. The jalapeño adds a nice pop of color to the golden, buttery bread.

To get a crispy crust on the bottom of the bread, I like to coat my pan in plenty of butter, heat it up, and literally "fry" the cornbread batter for a few minutes prior to baking it in the oven. I'm also a fan of adding whole corn kernels to the batter—I want my guests to know that they are getting the real thing! To create a nice presentation, I thinly slice some fresh jalapeño pepper, and arrange the slices over the top. The slices will just give into the bread, browning slightly while creating a rustic look that is a real crowd-pleaser when entertaining. Be sure to save any of those leftovers for my foolproof hangover cure: cornbread soaked in milk and topped with a drizzle of honey.

HANDS-ON 10 MIN. TOTAL 45 MIN.

SERVES 8-10

1 Preheat oven to 400°. Whisk together first 5 ingredients. Stir together buttermilk, eggs, and corn kernels in a separate bowl. Whisk buttermilk mixture and ½ cup melted butter into dry ingredients just until combined, being careful not to overwork batter.

2 Place a 9-inch cast-iron skillet over medium-high heat 2 minutes or until hot. Add 2 Tbsp. butter, and cook 1 minute or until melted. Pour batter into hot skillet, spreading to distribute evenly, and cook, without stirring, 2 minutes. Meanwhile, thinly slice jalapeño peppers, and arrange desired number of slices over batter.

3 Transfer skillet to oven, and bake at 400° for 25 minutes or until edges turn brown and cornbread pulls away from sides of skillet. Let stand 10 minutes before cutting into wedges and serving.

⇒ INGREDIENTS ⇐

1½ cups stone-ground white or yellow cornmeal
1 cup all-purpose flour
1 Tbsp. baking powder
1 tsp. kosher salt
2 Tbsp. sugar
1½ cups buttermilk
2 large eggs, beaten
1 cup fresh corn kernels
½ cup unsalted butter, melted
2 Tbsp. unsalted butter
2 jalapeño peppers

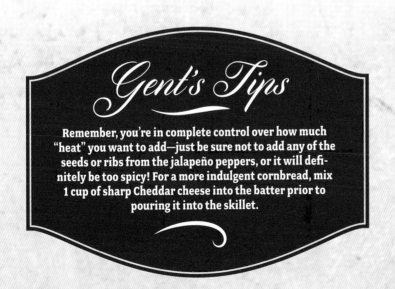

Gent's Tips

Remember, you're in complete control over how much "heat" you want to add—just be sure not to add any of the seeds or ribs from the jalapeño peppers, or it will definitely be too spicy! For a more indulgent cornbread, mix 1 cup of sharp Cheddar cheese into the batter prior to pouring it into the skillet.

Tried-and-True Buttermilk Biscuits

Buttermilk biscuits are as much a part of the Southern table as fried chicken, greens, and barbecue. Though the list of ingredients is quite short, perfecting the tender, flaky biscuits always takes a bit of practice.

When it comes to making the quintessential Southern biscuit, you must take three things to heart. One: keep the flour, butter, milk, and dough as cold as possible throughout the entire process. Two: don't overwork or overmix the dough; after kneading, fold the dough onto itself 3-4 times prior to patting it out for cutting to create flaky layers in the biscuit. Three: I like to cook my biscuits in a preheated cast-iron skillet, creating a crispy bottom.

HANDS-ON **10 MIN.** TOTAL **24 MIN.**

MAKES **6** BISCUITS

⇒ INGREDIENTS ⇐

Butter
2 cups self-rising soft-wheat flour
¼ tsp. kosher salt
5 Tbsp. very cold unsalted butter,
  cut into small cubes
¾ cup plus 1 Tbsp. very cold buttermilk

1 Preheat oven to 475°. Butter a 12-inch cast-iron skillet, and place in oven 5 minutes.

2 Meanwhile, combine flour and salt in a large bowl. Cut 5 Tbsp. butter into flour mixture with a pastry blender or fork until mixture resembles small peas. Stir in buttermilk with a fork just until dry ingredients are moistened.

3 Turn dough out onto a lightly floured surface; sprinkle top of dough with flour. Knead lightly 3-4 times, gradually adding additional self-rising flour as needed to prevent sticking. With floured hands, pat dough into a 1-inch-thick rectangle; dust top with flour. Fold dough over itself in 3 sections, starting with short end (as if folding a letter-size piece of paper).

4 Pat dough to 1-inch thickness. Cut dough into 5 biscuits using a 2½-inch round cutter. (Do not twist cutter; simply press down into dough to cut, and pull cutter straight up to release dough.) Gently reshape scraps, and cut out 1 more biscuit.

5 Place biscuits ½ inch apart in hot skillet. Bake at 475° for 12-14 minutes or until golden brown. Serve immediately.

Note: Tested with White Lily self-rising soft-wheat flour.

Bacon + Chive + White Cheddar Drop Biscuits

Every Sunday morning, Mama would prepare a big ole batch of drop biscuits for us to eat before we headed off to church. Like clockwork, we'd be just about to sit down to a table filled with jams and preserves, grits, scrambled eggs, and fresh-from-the-oven drop biscuits when an imposing figure would walk through our backyard. It was my childhood neighbor, Jimmy Breland, Jr., the son of Jim Breland, All-American center at Georgia Tech. Jimmy was the biggest kid in the neighborhood, and he had a healthy appetite! Mama had known our neighborly guest would stop by, so she always made plenty to go around the table. Simple memories and casual routines highlight my childhood. Even today, we still joke around with Jimmy and his family about the "Sunday ritual." It embodies my upbringing and my overall philosophy in the kitchen—great food is always at its finest when it's shared with loved ones and friends.

HANDS-ON 10 MIN. TOTAL **27 MIN.**
MAKES **2 DOZ.**

1 Place a small skillet over medium heat 2 minutes or until hot. Add bacon, and cook, stirring occasionally, 5 minutes or until crisp. Remove bacon using a slotted spoon, and drain on paper towels.

2 Preheat oven to 475°. Stir together flour and next 4 ingredients in a large bowl. Cut in cold butter with a pastry blender or fork until crumbly and mixture resembles small peas.

3 Gradually add milk, stirring until blended. Fold in cheese and chives. Crumble bacon into dough, stirring just until blended, and being careful not to overwork dough.

4 Drop dough by heaping tablespoonfuls 1 inch apart onto parchment paper–lined baking sheets. Bake at 475° for 12 minutes or until lightly browned. Serve immediately.

INGREDIENTS

4 hickory-smoked bacon slices, coarsely chopped
2 cups all-purpose flour
1½ Tbsp. baking powder
¼ tsp. garlic powder
¼ tsp. kosher salt
1 tsp. sugar
½ cup cold unsalted butter, cut into small pieces
1 cup plus 2 Tbsp. cold milk
1 cup (4 oz.) finely shredded sharp white Cheddar cheese
2 Tbsp. finely chopped fresh chives
Parchment paper

Jimmy, my sister Ashley, and me showing our school spirit one Sunday morning. As you can see, Jimmy was quite an imposing figure!

SWEET
+ SIMPLE

Sweet Cornbread + Fresh Fruit Trifle

Dessert should never be too complicated so I often rely on a few shortcuts. Such is the case in this recipe—I'm using a store-bought cornbread mix. Besides, Mama used this boxed mix all the time for her famous cornbread muffins. Some secrets are a cook's best friend.

An additional plus is that this dish is on the light side—something everybody can appreciate. I like to serve this dessert layered into individual glasses. And remember, it is best served à la minute, or on the fly, to keep the cornbread from becoming soggy.

HANDS-ON 15 MIN. TOTAL **1 HR.**

SERVES 4

⇒ INGREDIENTS ⇐

Vegetable cooking spray
1 (8½-oz.) package corn muffin mix
½ cup buttermilk
¼ cup butter, melted
1 large egg
3½ cups assorted fresh berries such as blackberries, raspberries, blueberries, and halved strawberries
⅓ cup sugar
⅓ cup black raspberry liqueur
1 cup whipping cream
1 cup vanilla Greek yogurt

1 Preheat oven to 400°. Lightly grease 8-inch square pan with cooking spray. Stir together first 4 ingredients in a large bowl until well blended. Pour batter into a prepared pan and bake at 400° for 15 minutes or until light golden brown and a wooden pick inserted in center comes out clean. Cool completely in pan on a wire rack (about 30 minutes).

2 Stir together berries, sugar, and liqueur in a medium bowl; gently mash about one-fourth of berries. Let stand, stirring occasionally, 30 minutes or until sugar dissolves.

3 Beat whipping cream at high speed with an electric mixer until stiff peaks form. Fold in yogurt.

4 Break cornbread into small pieces. Divide half of cornbread pieces among 4 (12-oz.) glasses. Top with half of berry mixture and half of whipped cream mixture. Repeat layers once, and serve immediately.

Note: Tested with Jiffy Corn Muffin Mix and Chambord liqueur.

Fresh Peach + Blueberry Cobbler

Since peaches and blueberries are abundant throughout the summer, fresh fruit cobbler finds its way onto my table at nearly every summertime dinner party. Combining peaches and blueberries is my favored version, although this recipe also works well with cherries, strawberries, and other fruits that ripen throughout the year.

The key to a great cobbler is the crust, which when done well is somewhat of a sweet, buttery biscuit. Like most of my recipes, I advise baking this in a cast-iron skillet, which provides even heat, as well as plenty of residual heat to keep the cobbler warm when served tableside, preferably with ice cream!

HANDS-ON 14 MIN. TOTAL **1 HR., 24 MIN.**

SERVES 8

1 Preheat oven to 375°. Toss together first 5 ingredients in a large bowl. Pour fruit mixture into a buttered 8-inch cast-iron skillet.

2 Stir together flour and next 2 ingredients in a small bowl. Cut ½ cup cold butter into flour mixture with a pastry blender or fork until crumbly and mixture resembles small peas. Add egg and vanilla, stirring with a fork until blended.

3 Dollop dough in 8 equal portions onto fruit mixture, making sure fruit mixture is mostly covered, but not spreading dough. Sprinkle dough with 1 tsp. sugar.

4 Bake at 375° for 40 minutes or until golden brown. Cool on a wire rack 30 minutes before serving. Serve warm.

⇒ INGREDIENTS ⇐

6 fresh peaches, peeled and cut into ½-inch slices (about 3 cups)

2 cups fresh blueberries

1 tsp. lemon zest

½ tsp. ground cinnamon

1 cup sugar

Butter

½ cup all-purpose flour

1 tsp. baking powder

Pinch of kosher salt

½ cup cold butter, cut into small pieces

1 large egg

½ tsp. vanilla extract

1 tsp. sugar

Grilled Georgia Peach Crumble

I don't have much of a sweet tooth. When it comes to eating meals, I'd rather have an extra helping of the main course than splurge on dessert. I also think serving a complicated dessert can often be quite a pain in the rear-end—I mean, who has hours to sit around and bake cakes all day? Not this guy. That's why I love this quick, simple recipe.

This is not one of those desserts that will make you feel like you got socked in the gut after you finish eating. Better yet, it's prepared on the grill, which means cleanup is easy. Though it might sound strange to throw a piece of fruit on the grill, it's actually one of the easiest ways to pull out the natural, caramel flavors from the sugar in the fruit. After creating beautiful grill marks, I like to add some crunchy granola for texture and serve the crumble alongside a dollop of cool, creamy Greek yogurt. It doesn't get any better.

HANDS-ON 10 MIN. TOTAL 27 MIN.
SERVES 4

INGREDIENTS

Vegetable cooking spray
4 fresh, ripe Georgia peaches, halved lengthwise (1½ lb.)
3 Tbsp. unsalted butter, cut into 8 cubes
2 Tbsp. light brown sugar
1 tsp. ground cinnamon
½ cup granola
2 cups vanilla fat-free Greek yogurt
Garnishes: ground cinnamon, fresh mint leaves

1 Coat cold cooking grate of grill with cooking spray, and place on grill. Light 1 side of grill, heating to 350°-400° (medium-high); light other side, heating to 250°-300° (low).

2 Coat peaches with cooking spray, and place peaches, cut sides down, on cooking grate over 350°-400° (medium-high) heat. Grill, covered with grill lid, 3 minutes. Rotate peaches 45°, and grill, covered with grill lid, 2 more minutes to create grill marks.

3 Turn peaches cut sides up, and transfer to other side of grill over 250°-300° (low) heat. Place a piece of butter in cavity of each peach half; sprinkle with sugar and cinnamon. Divide granola evenly among peaches; grill, covered with grill lid, 12 minutes.

4 Remove peaches from grill. Place 2 peach halves on each serving plate; spoon ½ cup Greek yogurt next to peaches on each plate. Serve immediately.

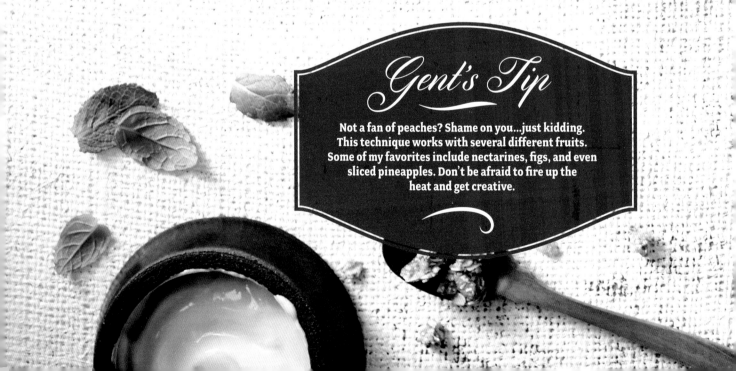

Gent's Tip

Not a fan of peaches? Shame on you...just kidding. This technique works with several different fruits. Some of my favorites include nectarines, figs, and even sliced pineapples. Don't be afraid to fire up the heat and get creative.

Mama's Showstopper

You haven't lived until you've eaten a bite of Mama's carrot cake. There's a running joke in my family that this cake is actually good for you—after all, the recipe calls for a pound of carrots, right? Ok, y'all, that might be stretching the truth a bit. This cake has been one of Mama's showstoppers for decades. In fact, it's probably her most requested recipe from all our family and friends.

Mama's Carrot Cake

The rich cake, topped off with crunchy pecans and silky smooth cream cheese icing, is absolutely worth praise. Served with hot coffee or tea, this dessert will become a family favorite.

HANDS-ON 25 MIN. TOTAL 2 HR.

SERVES 12

1 Prepare Carrot Cake: Preheat oven to 350°. Whisk together granulated sugar, 2 cups flour, and next 3 ingredients in a large bowl; make a well in center of mixture. Add eggs and oil; beat at medium speed with an electric mixer until blended. Add carrots, and beat 1 minute or until blended.

2 Lightly grease 3 (9-inch) round cake pans with cooking spray; line bottom of each pan with parchment paper; lightly grease paper with vegetable spray and flour. Spoon batter into prepared pans.

3 Bake at 350° for 25 minutes or until wooden pick inserted in center comes out clean. Cool in pans on wire racks 10 minutes. Remove from pans to wire racks; discard parchment paper. Cool completely (about 1 hour).

4 Prepare Cream Cheese Frosting: Beat cream cheese and butter at medium speed with an electric mixer 1 minute or until light and fluffy. Gradually add powdered sugar, ½ cup at a time, beating at low speed until blended after each addition. Add vanilla, and beat at low speed just until blended. Fold in pecans.

5 Spread frosting between layers and on top of cake (do not frost sides of cake). Serve immediately, or chill until ready to serve. Cover and refrigerate any leftover cake.

⇒ CARROT CAKE ⇐

2 cups granulated sugar
2 cups all-purpose flour
2 tsp. baking soda
2 tsp. ground cinnamon
1 tsp. kosher salt
4 large eggs
1½ cups canola oil
1 lb. carrots, peeled and finely grated
   (about 3 cups loosely packed)
Vegetable cooking spray
Parchment paper

⇒ CREAM CHEESE FROSTING ⇐

1 (8-oz.) package cream cheese, softened
½ cup unsalted butter, softened
1 (16-oz.) package powdered sugar
1 tsp. vanilla extract
1 cup chopped toasted pecans

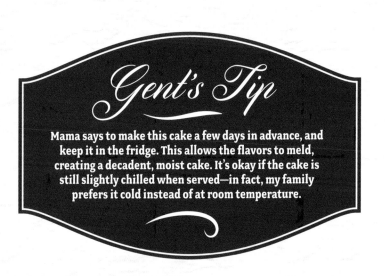

Gent's Tip

Mama says to make this cake a few days in advance, and keep it in the fridge. This allows the flavors to meld, creating a decadent, moist cake. It's okay if the cake is still slightly chilled when served—in fact, my family prefers it cold instead of at room temperature.

Sweet Potato Cupcakes

Admittedly, I'm over the whole cupcake craze of the last decade. Sure, cupcakes are great, but do we really need a cupcake shop or food truck on every corner? I'm all about a good cupcake, but damn…I think we've taken it a bit too far.

Well, I threw that whole rhetoric out the window the first time I tried a cupcake of the sweet potato variety. I was living in Nashville's historic Germantown district when a little mom-and-pop shop, The Cupcake Collection, opened up next door. I'd see folks lined up on Sundays after church waiting to buy these things by the dozen. Finally, despite my hesitation, I walked in and found a surprisingly humble, yet delicious assortment. After my first bite, I was hooked. Needless to say, Mrs. Mignon François and the rest of her family saw me quite a bit until I moved out of the neighborhood. Since that time, I had to come up with my own recipe to satisfy my cupcake craving.

HANDS-ON 20 MIN. TOTAL 1 HR.
MAKES 2 DOZ.

⇒ CUPCAKES ⇐

2 cups all-purpose flour
1 Tbsp. baking powder
½ tsp. kosher salt
1 tsp. ground cinnamon
1 (40-oz.) can sweet potatoes in syrup, drained and mashed (2¾ cups)
4 large eggs
1 cup vegetable oil
2 cups firmly packed light brown sugar
1 Tbsp. vanilla extract
24 paper baking cups

⇒ FROSTING ⇐

2 (8-oz.) packages cream cheese, softened
½ cup unsalted butter, softened
1 tsp. vanilla extract
2 cups powdered sugar

1 Prepare Cupcakes: Preheat oven to 375°. Whisk together flour and next 3 ingredients in a small bowl until blended. Whisk together mashed sweet potato and next 4 ingredients in a separate large bowl until blended. Whisk flour mixture into mashed sweet potato mixture just until blended.

2 Place paper baking cups in 2 (12-cup) muffin pans. Spoon batter into cups, filling three-fourths full.

3 Bake at 375° for 19-22 minutes or until a wooden pick inserted in center comes out clean. Cool in pans on wire racks 10 minutes. Remove from pans to wire rack, and cool completely (about 30 minutes).

4 Prepare Frosting: Beat cream cheese and butter at medium speed with an electric mixer until creamy. Add vanilla, and beat until blended. Gradually add powdered sugar, ½ cup at a time, beating at low speed until blended after each addition. Spread frosting on cupcakes.

Sweet Secret

For the life of me, I cannot think of one single family visit to Mississippi where Caramel Cake was not prepared and served by my grandmother Dorothy. Only years later did I learn from my Aunt Beth and Aunt Lynne that this famed dessert came from a box, shhh! So my grandmother saved a bit of time by focusing her efforts on the icing and allowing a little boxed magic to happen. That's right, she used a cake mix. No matter, the sweet, gooey, caramel icing and moist cake was always a favorite of mine—I often ate an extra helping of vegetables, with my parents' encouragement, knowing that such eating efforts would result in this fantastic dessert payoff.

Grandma Dorothy's Caramel Cake

I'm happy to share this family favorite for Caramel Cake with you and yours. The caramel icing, which is entirely made from scratch, is the star of the show, and is the reason why this dessert has been a family favorite for generations. Of course, if you have your own yellow cake recipe, feel free to use it, topping it all off with this classic icing.

HANDS-ON 32 MIN. **TOTAL 2 HR., 12 MIN.**

SERVES 8-10

1 Lightly grease 3 (8-inch) round cake pans with cooking spray; flour pans. Prepare cake mix batter according to package directions, stirring in 1 cup water, ½ cup oil, and 3 eggs as directed. Spoon batter into prepared pans, and bake as directed. Cool in pans on wire racks 10 minutes; remove from pans to wire racks, and cool completely (about 1 hour).

2 After cakes have cooled completely, sprinkle ½ cup sugar into a 2-qt. stainless steel or aluminum saucepan or stainless steel skillet. Cook over medium-low heat, shaking pan frequently, 6 minutes or until sugar melts and turns a light golden brown.

3 Meanwhile, combine remaining 2 cups sugar and cream in a heavy 3-qt. saucepan. Bring to a light boil over medium heat, stirring occasionally.

4 Pour melted sugar into cream mixture, and cook, stirring often, about 10 minutes or until a candy thermometer registers 235° (soft ball stage—see Gent's Tip below). Remove from heat, and stir in vanilla and butter until butter melts and mixture is smooth. Cool, stirring occasionally, 30 minutes or until thickened and spreading consistency (about 120°).

5 Working quickly, immediately spread frosting between layers and on top and sides of cake. Cool 1 hour or until set before serving.

⇒ INGREDIENTS ⇐

Vegetable cooking spray
1 (16.25-oz.) package yellow cake mix
½ cup vegetable oil
3 large eggs
2½ cups sugar, divided
½ pint heavy cream
1 tsp. vanilla extract
3 Tbsp. unsalted butter

Gent's Tip

To test for soft ball stage, just put a cup of cold water next to your stove when you boil the mixture. Using a spoon, add a drop or so of the caramel mixture into the water. If it thins out in the water, dump out, replace the water, and continue cooking the mixture. Softball stage is reached when the mixture forms a soft, congealed ball in the water.

Goo Goo Cluster Brownies à la Mode

As an adopted Nashvillian, it would be a crime to not pay homage to one of the South's greatest confectionary creations—the Goo Goo Cluster. Created in Nashville by the Standard Candy Company, this beloved treat has been a favorite the world over for more than a century. In fact, the nutty, caramel, chocolate, and marshmallow combination bar was the first of its kind, standing out amongst a pack of all-chocolate bars. Throughout the Great Depression, Goo Goo Clusters were hawked as "a nourishing lunch for a nickel." My, oh my, how times they have changed.

In any event, I like to make up a big batch of brownies, fortified with this delicious treat, and serve them warm with a hearty helping of vanilla ice cream on the side. Since my wife, Callie, and I are often entertaining, this happens to be one of our go-to desserts to serve friends. Honestly, for the time, taste, and nostalgia—this dessert is hard to beat.

HANDS-ON 10 MIN. TOTAL **1 HR., 40 MIN.**

MAKES **9** BROWNIES

INGREDIENTS

Vegetable cooking spray
3 Original Goo Goo Clusters
1 cup sugar
½ cup all-purpose flour
⅓ cup unsweetened cocoa
½ tsp. baking powder
¼ tsp. kosher salt, divided
½ cup vegetable oil
2 large eggs
Vanilla ice cream

1 Preheat oven to 350°. Line bottom and sides of an 8-inch square pan with aluminum foil, allowing 2 inches to extend over sides; lightly grease foil with cooking spray. Coarsely chop Goo Goo Clusters into bite-size pieces to equal 1¼ cups.

2 Whisk together sugar, next 3 ingredients, and ⅛ tsp. salt in a large bowl until blended. Make a well in center of mixture; add oil and eggs to well, and stir until batter is blended and smooth. Fold three-fourths of chopped candy into batter. Pour into prepared pan.

3 Bake at 350°, on center oven rack, for 30 minutes or until a wooden pick inserted in center comes out clean. Remove from oven, and immediately sprinkle with remaining ⅛ tsp. salt and remaining chopped candy. Cool completely on a wire rack (about 1 hour).

4 Lift brownies from pan, using foil sides as handles. Gently remove foil, and cut into 9 squares. To serve, reheat brownies, and serve warm with ice cream.

Note: Tested with Mayfield Homemade Vanilla Ice Cream. You can find Goo Goo Clusters at Cracker Barrel Old Country Stores, Hobby Lobby, and other retailers, as well as online at www.googoo.com.

Saint Rita's Cakes

Cooking ain't just for pleasure in my family, in fact, it's all business for my Aunt Jeanne. Her famous pound cakes, known as Saint Rita's Cakes, are a huge hit all over the great city of Atlanta.

Jeanne started baking cakes in her home and gifting them to friends and family throughout the year. After some encouragement from the local proprietor at Atlanta's famed Lucy's Market, she began making her cakes available to the public. It wasn't long before the word got out, and the rest, as we say, is history.

Aunt Jeanne's Traditional Southern Pound Cake

This classic recipe is inspired by Aunt Jeanne's famous cakes. I always enjoy a slice of pound cake on slow, weekend mornings, when I have time to sit around with my wife, Callie, reading *The Tennessean* while enjoying a cup or two of Community Coffee. Extra props to those who like to dunk their cake in their coffee—that's how I do it, too.

HANDS-ON 15 MIN.   TOTAL 3 HR., 15 MIN.

SERVES 10

1 Preheat oven to 325°. Grease a 10-inch Bundt pan with shortening, and sprinkle with 2 Tbsp. flour, shaking out any excess.

2 Whisk together 3 cups flour, baking powder, and salt.

3 Beat butter and vanilla at medium speed with a heavy-duty electric stand mixer until creamy. Gradually add sugar, ½ cup at a time, beating about 3 minutes or until fluffy. Add eggs, 1 at a time, beating just until blended after each addition.

4 Add flour mixture to butter mixture alternately with half-and-half, beginning and ending with flour mixture. Beat at low speed just until blended after each addition. Pour batter into prepared pan, smoothing top of batter with a spatula.

5 Bake at 325° on middle oven rack for 1 hour-1 hour, 5 minutes, or until a long wooden pick inserted in center comes out clean. Cool cake in pan on a wire rack 10 minutes; remove from pan to wire rack, and cool completely (about 2 hours).

INGREDIENTS

- 2 Tbsp. shortening
- 3 cups plus 2 Tbsp. all-purpose flour, divided
- 1 tsp. baking powder
- ¼ tsp. kosher salt
- 1 cup unsalted butter, softened
- 1 Tbsp. vanilla extract
- 2½ cups granulated sugar
- 6 large eggs, at room temperature
- ¾ cup half-and-half

Gent's Tip

This ain't my tip—it's my Aunt Jeanne's. Although this cake is delicious served on its own, it can also be glazed for even more deliciousness. Stir together 1 cup powdered sugar, 1 tsp. half-and-half, and 2 Tbsp. fresh lemon juice in a bowl until creamy. Drizzle glaze over cooled cake, and let stand 30 minutes before serving.

Hot + Ready Beignets + Sorghum-Cayenne Drizzle

Nowadays, beignet recipes are ubiquitous, but I like to up the ante by serving these as a dessert with my sweet-and-spicy sorghum and cayenne drizzle. This is my coup de grâce when I'm looking to finish a great meal with a one-two punch! I like to prep this dough a day in advance, allowing me to slip off into the kitchen after dinner to quickly deep-fry these guys and return to plenty of oohs and ahhhs.

HANDS-ON 40 MIN. TOTAL 4 HR., 40 MIN.

MAKES ABOUT 30 BEIGNETS

1 Combine yeast, warm water, and granulated sugar in a 1-cup glass measuring cup; let stand 5 minutes. Combine yeast mixture, salt, and next 2 ingredients in bowl of a heavy-duty electric stand mixer or large bowl. Gradually add half of flour, beating at low speed or whisking just until blended after each addition. Add shortening, beating or whisking until blended. Gradually add remaining flour, a little at a time, beating at low speed or whisking just until blended after each addition.

2 Turn dough out onto a well-floured surface. Knead dough, using heel of your hand to push dough away from your body, turning counterclockwise, and folding in half; knead about 10 times or until smooth and elastic. Place dough in a large bowl well-greased with shortening, turning to grease top. Cover and chill 4-24 hours.

3 Turn dough out onto a well-floured surface. Lightly flour rolling pin, and roll dough into a 10- x 12-inch rectangle (about ½-inch thick). Cut into 2-inch squares. Transfer to a floured baking sheet.

4 Place a 12-inch cast-iron skillet over medium-high heat. Add peanut oil to a depth of 1½ inches, and heat to 350°. Fry 4-6 beignets at a time, 1½ minutes, per side or until golden. (Beignets should puff and begin to brown when they touch the hot oil.) Carefully transfer cooked beignets to a paper towel–lined plate to drain. Keep warm.

5 Stir together sorghum syrup and cayenne pepper; drizzle over beignets. Sprinkle with powdered sugar, and serve immediately.

INGREDIENTS

1 (¼-oz.) envelope active dry yeast
¾ cup warm water (between 105°-110°)
3 Tbsp. granulated sugar
¼ tsp. kosher salt
2 large eggs, beaten
½ cup evaporated milk
3½ cups all-purpose flour
¼ cup shortening, cut into pieces
Shortening
Peanut oil
½ cup sorghum syrup
1 tsp. ground cayenne pepper
Powdered sugar

COCKTAILS + CURIOSITIES

Hand-Squeezed Lemonade

Fresh, hand-squeezed lemonade—just saying those words puts a smile on my face. From Greensboro, North Carolina, to Dyersburg, Tennessee, and Lake Charles, Louisiana, you'll find a favorite version of this beloved drink throughout the South. Think of the roadside lemonade stand. Kids selling cupfuls of homemade lemonade for less than a buck to everyone who passes by.

This tradition provides a first glimpse into the world of entrepreneurship for the young'uns—and trust me, your stuff better be good if you want to outsell all the other kids in your neighborhood.

No powdered mixes here—we're making this classic with fresh, hand-squeezed lemons. As Daddy always said, "Don't wish for it—work for it!"

HANDS-ON **6 MIN.** TOTAL **6 MIN.**
MAKES **7 CUPS**

⇉ INGREDIENTS ⇇

4 lemons
1 cup hot water
1 cup sugar
4 cups cold water

1 Cut lemons in half. Squeeze juice from lemons into a measuring cup to equal 1 cup. Pour lemon juice through a fine wire-mesh strainer into a bowl; discard pulp and seeds.

2 Stir together hot water and sugar in a large pitcher until sugar dissolves. Stir in lemon juice and cold water. Serve over ice.

Cajun Lemonade

Sweet and spicy, with plenty of alcohol—now we're talking. This refreshing cocktail is sure to tantalize your taste buds with plenty of heat, while serving up a shot of booze to take the edge off. Similar to margarita glasses rimmed with salt, I like to rim the glasses for this drink with savory Creole seasoning to keep this cocktail festive.

HANDS-ON **5 MIN.** TOTAL **11 MIN.**
SERVES **1**

⇉ INGREDIENTS ⇇

Lemon wedge
Creole seasoning
¼ cup vodka
½ cup Hand-Squeezed Lemonade
  (above)*
¼ cup sparkling water or club soda
Garnishes: fresh basil sprig, very thin
  jalapeño pepper slices, thin lemon slices

*Bottled fresh lemonade, such as Simply
Lemonade, may be substituted.

1 Rub rim of a highball glass with lemon wedge. Pour Creole seasoning on a plate, and dip glass into seasoning; shake off any excess. Fill glass with ice.

2 Add vodka and lemonade, stirring until blended; gently stir in sparkling water.

Cajun Lemonade

NOLA Sazerac

It's only appropriate that one of the world's oldest and most famous cocktails comes from one of the South's greatest cities—New Orleans, aka NOLA. The Sazerac, which dates back to the early 1800s, inherited its name from the brand of cognac first used to prepare this classic—I substitute rye whiskey for the cognac.

The key to perfecting this cocktail is not so much the ingredients, as it is the preparation, "flavoring" the glass with a bit of absinthe or Herbsaint prior to pouring in the whiskey mixture. The result is a drink beloved by many, so much so that it has gained the status as the "official" cocktail for the city in which it was born.

HANDS-ON **4 MIN.** TOTAL **4 MIN.**

SERVES **1**

1 Fill an old-fashioned glass with ice and water; let stand to chill glass.

2 Meanwhile, muddle bitters with sugar in a cocktail shaker. Add rye whiskey; cover with lid, and shake vigorously until blended.

3 Pour ice water out of chilled glass, and pour in liqueur; swirl to coat inside of glass, and discard any excess liqueur. Pour rye whiskey mixture into chilled, coated glass.

Note: Tested with Herbsaint or absinthe anise liqueur.

⋛ INGREDIENTS ⋚

2-3 dashes Peychaud's bitters
1 cube sugar*
6 Tbsp. rye whiskey
½ tsp. anise liqueur
Garnish: lemon peel

*1 tsp. simple syrup may be substituted.

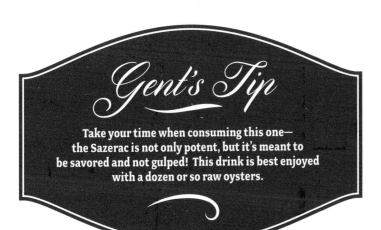

Gent's Tip

Take your time when consuming this one—the Sazerac is not only potent, but it's meant to be savored and not gulped! This drink is best enjoyed with a dozen or so raw oysters.

Bacon Old-Fashioned

When it comes to bacon, we Southerners are always getting creative. Like, say, adding bacon flavor to bourbon. That's what gives this traditional cocktail a makeover.

Here's the deal: Cook 4 to 5 strips of your favorite hickory-smoked bacon in a skillet. Eat that delicious bacon—mmm. Pour 1 (750-milliliter) bottle of your favorite bourbon and the bacon drippings from skillet into a 4-cup glass measuring cup; let stand at room temperature for 24 hours. Pop the measuring cup into the freezer for a couple of hours. Pull it out, and skim off the bacon fat (it will congeal and separate from the alcohol). Pour the ice-cold bourbon through a cheese-cloth-lined strainer into a glass jar to remove any particles. Your bourbon is now flavored with the smoky bacon fat for use in all of your favorite cocktails.

HANDS-ON 5 MIN. TOTAL 5 MIN.

SERVES 1

⇒ INGREDIENTS ⇐

1 sugar cube or ½ tsp. granulated sugar
2-3 dashes Angostura bitters
¼ cup bacon-infused bourbon
Garnishes: bacon strips, orange peel
   strip, or maraschino cherry

1 Muddle sugar, bitters, and 1 tsp. water in an old-fashioned glass to release flavors and blend ingredients. Swirl sugar mixture to coat inside of glass. Add 1 large ice cube, and pour bourbon over ice. Serve immediately.

Classic Mint Julep

Your life is not complete without seeing the horses run the famous track at Churchill Downs. My first trip to the Kentucky Derby was not filled with great expensive hats and fancy suits, rather I threw $40 into the massive coffers along with thousands of others to witness the event from the infield. Although I hardly saw the race, I'm quite certain that the true main event takes place in this infield area—the stench of booze, cigarettes, and horse manure is quite unique.

After one too many mint juleps, my buddies and I paid a school bus driver (not kidding) to take us through the city of Mockingbird Valley and on to Glenview to attend a Derby party thrown by Louisville's elite. We were dirty, sun-tanned, and improperly dressed—but that didn't stop us from rubbing elbows with the rich and famous. When asked what box we sat in for the race, my buddy Miller confidently told the group that we'd been sitting in the "inner track area." (Ah, way to gussy up that one, Miller.) At that moment, I knew it was time to head to the kitchen to pour a traveler—one more mint julep for the road—before we were properly sent on our way from that particular Kentucky home.

HANDS-ON **5 MIN.** TOTAL **5 MIN.**

SERVES **1**

1 Muddle mint leaves and sugar in a chilled julep cup or cocktail glass to release flavors. Pack cup tightly with crushed ice; add bourbon and mint sprig.

Note: Tested with Angel's Envy bourbon.

⩾ INGREDIENTS ⩽

4 fresh mint leaves
2 tsp. powdered sugar
Crushed ice
3 oz. bourbon
Fresh mint sprig

Georgia Peach

Though you'll find several variations of this cocktail at bars throughout the South, one thing is certain... this is the taste of Georgia wrapped up into one tasty sip! My variation is less sweet than the traditional cocktail, focusing on the subtle peach flavor and spirits—imagine that.

Looking to impress that lovely lady down at the end of the bar? Send one of these her way, and spin a tune from The Allman Brothers Band on the jukebox. You're welcome.

HANDS-ON **2 MIN.**　TOTAL **2 MIN.**
SERVES **1**

⇉ INGREDIENTS ⇇

3 Tbsp. vodka

1 Tbsp. peach schnapps

¼ cup fresh orange juice

¼ cup cranberry juice cocktail

Garnish: orange twist or peach slice

1 Combine first 4 ingredients in a cocktail shaker; add ice. Cover with lid, and shake until thoroughly chilled (about 30 seconds). Strain into a cocktail glass. Serve immediately.

Bourbon Street Hurricane

During wartime production in the 1940s, some distilleries in the United States produced alcohol to use as torpedo fuel rather than alcoholic beverages. This meant that tavern owners were subject to shortages of some of the most popular spirits, including whiskey. As the story goes, that was the case at legendary Pat O'Brien's on Bourbon Street in New Orleans, and head bartender Louis Culligan created the Hurricane to allure patrons while making use of a less-popular, yet abundant spirit—dark rum.

Rum heavy and served in a hurricane lamp-shaped glass, this drink soon became a favorite among sailors—and later tourists—in and around the French Quarter. Prepared properly, this drink satisfies while taking the edge off a hot, humid Louisiana afternoon.

HANDS-ON **2 MIN.** TOTAL **2 MIN.**

SERVES **1**

1 Combine first 3 ingredients in a cocktail shaker; add ice. Cover with lid, and shake vigorously until thoroughly chilled (about 10 seconds). Fill a large glass with crushed ice. Strain mixture into glass.

Note: Tested with Ceres Passion Fruit Juice 100% Fruit Juice.

≥ INGREDIENTS ≤

¼ cup dark rum
½ cup passion fruit juice
2 Tbsp. fresh squeezed lemon juice
Crushed ice
Garnishes: orange slice,
   maraschino cherry

Sweet Sun Tea

Needless to say, it gets pretty hot in Georgia during the summer months. As it is, the Atlanta moniker "Hotlanta" is certainly well deserved.

Mama would often make use of the high outside temps and bright sunlight to brew up a batch of sweet sun tea, keeping the stove, and thereby her kitchen, cool. Since we often had fresh mint growing in our backyard, we'd commonly add it to the tea to give it a bit of sweet, herbal flavor. When poured over ice and chilled, there's no better way to fight back the heat of a Southern summer.

HANDS-ON **5 MIN.** TOTAL **3 HR., 15 MIN.**

MAKES **8 CUPS**

⋛ INGREDIENTS ⋚

2 family-size tea bags
Sugar
Garnish: fresh mint sprigs

1 Fill a glass jug with 2 qt. distilled water; add tea bags. Cover tightly with lid, and place in direct sunlight for 3-5 hours.

2 Discard tea bags. Stir tea, and serve over ice. Add sugar to taste.

Gent's Sweet Tea

There's nothing better than kicking back on a large veranda, sipping a glass of refreshing iced sweet tea, while taking in the beautiful Southern landscape. Well, there actually is something better—sipping sweet tea that's spiked with a bit of whiskey. I perfected this classic recipe at many "dry" weddings by emptying my flask into iced sweet tea at the reception. Hey, say what you will, but the party (and my dancing) is always better after I've had a few of these. Follow my steps (above) to make perfect iced tea, and from there we'll spike it up a bit.

HANDS-ON **5 MIN.** TOTAL **5 MIN.**

SERVES **1**

⋛ INGREDIENTS ⋚

2 mint leaves
2 oz. Tennessee whiskey
6 oz. Sweet Sun Tea
1½ tsp. fresh lemon juice
Garnishes: fresh mint sprig,
  lemon wedge

1 Muddle mint leaves in a cocktail shaker to release flavors. Add whiskey and next 2 ingredients. Cover with lid, and shake vigorously 10 seconds. Pour over ice in a large glass.

The Brown Derby

Time to sweeten your daddy's bourbon with honey and add some refreshing grapefruit juice to re-create the classic Brown Derby. This drink was the cocktail of choice for the glamorous Hollywood crowd of the 1930s. For those ladies out there who won't typically drink bourbon, give this a try. You'll be singing "Blue Moon of Kentucky" after the first sip.

HANDS-ON 5 MIN.   TOTAL 5 MIN.
SERVES 1

—⟩ INGREDIENTS ⟨—

¼ cup Kentucky bourbon
¼ cup grapefruit juice
1 tsp. clover honey
Garnish: grapefruit peel strip

1 Combine all ingredients in a cocktail shaker; add ice. Cover with lid, and shake vigorously 10 seconds. Fill a cocktail glass with crushed ice. Strain mixture into glass.

SAVANNAH BEE COMPANY

Owner and curator of the Savannah Bee Company Ted Dennard became fascinated with bees after a chance encounter with Roy Hightower, an elderly beekeeper. Ted went on to teach beekeeping to folks in Central America through the Peace Corps. Upon returning to Savannah, he quit his day job and launched his amazing honey business. Ted's passion for his business and his bees is obvious. It's a contagious passion that carries over into his fine honeys, skin care products, and honey-based spirits (see page 278).

Pickled Okra Bloody Mary

In my opinion, the best brunch cocktail by far and away is a Bloody Mary. Whether serving as a hangover cure or simply a lift on a casual weekend morning, I love the spicy combo of tomato juice, vodka, and other select accoutrements. Since I like spicy foods, my version calls for both Tabasco and horseradish. The beauty of this drink is that you can completely personalize it—just go a little easy or heavy on the spice based on each person's preference.

My wife, Callie, and I like to make up a big Bloody Mary bar for brunches with each ingredient laid out on the countertop so folks can experiment and make their own drinks. Trust me—invite your friends over, make a Bloody Mary bar, cook up a delicious brunch, and many, many good times will definitely follow.

HANDS-ON 5 MIN. TOTAL 5 MIN.
SERVES 1

⇛ INGREDIENTS ⇚

¼ cup plus 2 Tbsp. tomato juice
3 Tbsp. vodka
1 tsp. fresh lime juice
¼ tsp. celery salt
¼ tsp. freshly ground black pepper
2 dashes of Worcestershire sauce
2 dashes of hot sauce
½ tsp. prepared horseradish
Garnishes: Pickled Okra (page 263), lime wedge

1 Combine first 8 ingredients in a cocktail shaker. Cover with lid, and shake vigorously until blended (about 30 seconds). Pour into a tall glass filled with ice. Serve immediately.

Note: Tested with Tabasco hot sauce.

Gent's Tip

For the best flavor, I prefer to give the pickled okra (used here as a garnish) at least 1 week to cure before serving.

Pickled Okra

These fellas make for quick, convenient snacks, as well as a great garnish for that Pickled Okra Bloody Mary. Crisp, tangy, and delicious—I love canning a bunch of these early in the season when okra is young and tender. Unlike making Icebox Dill Pickles (page 266), I sterilize everything to ensure that these jars can be stored, without refrigeration, up to one year's time. Be meticulous about keeping everything clean throughout the process.

HANDS-ON **38 MIN.** TOTAL **50 MIN.,** PLUS 1 DAY FOR STANDING

MAKES **8** 1 PT. JARS

1 Trim stems from okra (do not cut off ends). Peel garlic cloves.

2 Place 8 (1-pt.) glass canning jars in a large stockpot or canner, and add water to cover. Bring water to a rolling boil over medium-high heat; boil 2 minutes. Meanwhile, place lids (always use new lids) and bands in a large saucepan. Using a ladle, cover lids and bands with hot water from stockpot (to soften gaskets on lids). Remove stockpot from heat. Let jars, lids, and bands stand in hot water 10 minutes.

3 Meanwhile, bring vinegar, 1¼ cups water, and salt to a boil in a large saucepan over medium-high heat. Reduce heat to medium-low, and simmer 5 minutes.

4 Remove jars from stockpot, 1 at a time, using a jar lifter. Place jars 2 inches apart on a work surface. Place 2 peeled garlic cloves and 1 sliced pepper in each jar. Tightly pack okra in jars vertically in 2 layers (first layer packed with stems down, and second with stems up), filling to 1 inch from top. Add 1 tsp. dill seeds to each jar.

5 Pour hot vinegar mixture over okra mixture in jars, filling to ½ inch from top. Wipe rims of filled jars. Cover at once with lids, and screw on bands. The heat from vinegar mixture should seal jars; you will hear a popping noise when jars are sealed. Let jars stand at room temperature for 24 hours before confirming seals.

6 Test seals of jars by pressing centers of lids; if lids do not pop, jars are properly sealed. Store in a cool, dark place at room temperature up to 1 year; refrigerate after opening. If lids are not sealed, refrigerate and use within 1 month.

⋛ INGREDIENTS ⋚

3 lb. fresh, young okra, washed
16 garlic cloves
8 (1-pt.) glass canning jars
5 cups white vinegar (5% acidity)
½ cup kosher salt
8 fresh Fresno hot chile peppers, thinly sliced into rings
8 tsp. dill seeds

THAD COCKRELL

O ne six-pack Yazoo Pale Ales. Two-dozen
Apalachicola oysters. One pound locally
smoked pork belly. Sliced Kenny's
Farmhouse Cheddar cheese. Hank Williams.
These are the ingredients that one of Nashville's
humblest songwriters, Thad Cockrell, and I have
decided upon for an afternoon in Nashville's
buzzing 12 South neighborhood. Unbeknownst
to us, our ingredients and conversation led us
to solve one of life's unique conundra. Hot
Sauce : Cooking :: Songwriting : Music. Allow
me to explain.

I first met Thad after church service, while
attending an impromptu brunch thrown by our
friends Chuck and Pap Shirock, a husband/wife

musical duo worth checking out. It was Thad's
Green Truth hot sauce that caught my attention
when the potluck dishes were slowly passed
around the table. I couldn't get enough of the
tangy, slightly sweet, back-off a bit, cut you to
the bone, soothing flavor. I heard the sirens'
song calling, and I couldn't resist dousing every
bite of my food in this delicious nectar. As it
turns out, Thad is known for other talents
besides his sauce.

The son of a Baptist pastor, Thad has a 'true
country' musical style. His first EP, recorded in
one day, was met with critical acclaim, and his
alt-country, no depression songs have contin-
ued to garner even more credits and accolades.
Thad now fronts LEAGUES, a popular rock band
gaining national attention. He and I joke about
Thad's success on Top 40 radio this 'late' in his
career, acknowledging that substance, talent,
and great songs will always prevail.

The same could be said about cooking
because a meal is only as good as its ingredients. Cooking and songwriting share many
commonalities. To write a recipe—concept,
ingredients, and methods—is much the same as
writing a great song—title, verse, hook/chorus,
and bridge. Same goes for being a gentleman;
one must live out the words and ideals in daily
action and practice—being a man of his word,
of honor, of tradition, and of humility—all of
which describe Thad to a T.

Hot sauces carry gentle nuances of flavor,
bold punches of heat, while also harkening back
through tastes to remind us of past occasions.
I'll be damned if I don't get that same experience when I listen to a great song. Love which
stings, nights that never end, memories and
feelings that last a lifetime—all wrapped up
in one single bite, or three minutes, thirty
seconds. Genius.

It's only appropriate that I share the following
recipe for you to create your own memories,
either through song or tastes. Cheers to you,
Thad.

The Green Truth

The key to a great hot sauce is balance. It's the delicate nuance of heat, flavor, acidity, and bite. This variation smartly relies on avocado, allowing its rich, creamy texture to ensure all of the ingredients meld together. It also adds to its vibrant green color. I serve this sauce most often as an accompaniment to thick cuts of blackened fish or poultry. It's also incredibly delicious when served as a dipping sauce for a thinly sliced skirt steak, hot off the grill.

HANDS-ON 20 MIN. **TOTAL 20 MIN.**
MAKES 2 CUPS

1 Process all ingredients in a blender or food processor until smooth, about 30 seconds, stopping to scrape down sides as needed. Cover and chill until ready to serve.

⋛ INGREDIENTS ⋚

7 large jalapeño peppers, stemmed and cut in half (about 11½ oz.)

1 habanero pepper, stemmed and cut in half (about ¾ oz.)

2 medium garlic cloves

1½ Tbsp. fresh lime juice

¼ cup olive or vegetable oil

½ avocado, peeled and seeded

1 tsp. table salt

Icebox Dill Pickles

Whenever you open up my refrigerator at home, you will find some sort of pickled concoction. Pickling vegetables is somewhat like a science experiment—once you perfect the brine, it's just a matter of adding jolts of flavor with fresh herbs, aromatics, and spice.

I find that a lot of folks tend to be fearful when it comes to pickling and preserving—and for good reason. The traditional process relies on sterilization and exact methods to ensure food can be stored for long periods without refrigeration. But these pickles are prepared quickly and stored safely in the fridge up to a month or so. It's best to use cucumbers just pulled from the vine (ask the farmer who harvested them) to keep the pickles nice and crisp. Let's get real...nobody wants a soggy pickle! These make a healthy snack, a nice addition to a crudité or antipasto platter, or gracing a burger.

HANDS-ON **10 MIN.**   TOTAL **10 MIN.,** PLUS **3** DAYS FOR CHILLING

MAKES **2** 1 PT. JARS

INGREDIENTS

1 cup white vinegar (5% acidity)
1½ tsp. sugar
2¼ tsp. kosher salt
5 whole black peppercorns
6 garlic cloves
1¼ lb. Kirby cucumbers,
   cut into ½-inch-thick slices
½ jalapeño pepper, cut in half
   and seeded
2 Tbsp. fresh dill weed, coarsely chopped
2 (1-pt.) glass canning jars

1 Bring first 4 ingredients and ¾ cup water to a boil in a small saucepan over medium-high heat. Reduce heat to low, and simmer 5 minutes.

2 Meanwhile, smash garlic cloves using flat side of a knife. Divide cucumber slices, jalapeño pepper, dill weed, and smashed garlic between 2 (1-pt.) glass canning jars; tightly pack ingredients, layering to distribute garlic and dill weed throughout jars, and fill to ½ inch from top. Pour hot vinegar mixture over cucumber mixture, filling to ½ inch from top (be sure all ingredients are covered with liquid). Cover at once with lids, and screw on bands. Chill 3 days before serving to allow flavors to meld.

Pickled Radishes

The French might be known for their love and use of radishes, but the vegetable grows quite well in our rich Southern soils. Crunchy, starchy, and a bit bitter, while also slightly sweet, these vegetables are finding their way into salads and entrées throughout the land.

I like radishes best when they are pickled. The pickling solution takes out much of the bitterness, while keeping everything crisp and slightly sour to nicely balance fatty proteins or provide a tasty addition to a plate of cheese and charcuterie. Much like Spicy Sweet Pickled Carrots (page 269), they are ready to eat within 24 hours, and they keep up to a month when stored in the fridge.

HANDS-ON **12 MIN.** TOTAL **57 MIN.,** PLUS **1 DAY FOR CHILLING**

MAKES **2** 1 PT. JARS

1 Combine first 3 ingredients and 1 cup water in a small saucepan, and bring to a boil over medium-high heat. Reduce heat to low, and simmer 5 minutes.

2. Meanwhile, smash garlic cloves using flat side of a knife. Tightly pack sliced radishes, peppercorns, and smashed garlic into 2 (1-pint) glass canning jars, filling to ½ inch from top. Pour hot vinegar mixture over radish mixture in jars, filling to ½ inch from top. Cover at once with lids, and screw on bands. Cool to room temperature (about 45 minutes). Chill 1 day before serving.

⊰ INGREDIENTS ⊱

1 cup white wine vinegar

3 tsp. kosher salt

1 Tbsp. sugar

2 garlic cloves

1 lb. radishes, very thinly sliced (about 3¼ cups)

10 whole black peppercorns

2 (1-pt.) glass canning jars

Spicy Sweet Pickled Carrots

I usually surprise my guests with these sweet, yet very spicy carrots as a way to open up my friends' palates. Habanero peppers add tons of heat, while also lending their unique flavor to bring out some of the natural sweetness and sugar in the carrots. These carrots tempt you with their crunchy sweet flavors, but there's almost—and

I said almost—just enough heat to stop you from eating another. These are surprisingly good when served with hummus or buttermilk Ranch dressing—I find that both dips balance out the spice while ramping up the flavor in a way that's hard to describe. You can refrigerate pickled carrots in an airtight container up to a month.

HANDS-ON **8 MIN.** TOTAL **8 MIN.,** PLUS **1** DAY FOR CHILLING

MAKES **2** 1 PT. JARS

1 Bring first 4 ingredients and 1¼ cups water to a boil in a small saucepan over medium-high heat. Reduce heat to low, and simmer 5 minutes.

2 Pack carrots vertically in 2 layers in 2 (1-pt.) glass canning jars, filling to ½ inch from top, and placing garlic and habanero between layers. Pour hot vinegar mixture into jars, filling to ½ inch from top. Cover at once with lids, and screw on bands. Chill at least 1 day before serving.

INGREDIENTS

1¼ cups apple cider vinegar
¼ cup sugar
1 Tbsp. plus 1½ tsp. kosher salt
10 coriander seeds
1 lb. carrots, peeled and cut into
  3- x ½-inch pieces
2 (1-pt.) glass canning jars
2 garlic cloves, halved
1 habanero pepper, quartered

Gent's Tip

Whenever I've got a jar of a canned concoction in my fridge, I'm always sure to label everything with the date, along with its contents. These spicy guys are sure to wake up your taste buds if you think they are just plain carrots! Spend a bit of time to label your jars to ensure they are always okay to eat.

Fresh Strawberry Preserves

June strawberries produce a once-a-year harvest that marks the start to my summer. Much like homegrown tomatoes, backyard strawberries always taste better than anything you'll find in the supermarket.

Instead of spending tons of time and adding preservatives to the strawberries, per a traditional method, I like to utilize a simple process and technique that keeps them for a few weeks in the fridge. Besides, I find that once I can them, they don't last long! I use these preserves on top of my morning drop biscuits and as a nice complement to a fruit-and-cheese platter for entertaining and snacks—the preserves are darn good.

HANDS-ON **8 MIN.** TOTAL **8 MIN.,** PLUS 1 DAY FOR CHILLING

MAKES **5½** 1 PT. JARS

⋛ INGREDIENTS ⋚

2 lb. fresh strawberries,
  trimmed and halved
3 cups sugar
2 Tbsp. plus 1½ tsp. fresh lemon juice
  (1 lemon)
1/16 tsp. kosher salt
5 (½-pt.) hot sterilized glass canning jars

1 Place strawberries in a large mixing bowl. Using a potato masher, mash strawberries to equal about 4 cups, leaving desired amount of small chunks. Transfer mashed strawberries to a Dutch oven, and place over low heat.

2 Add sugar and next 2 ingredients; cook, stirring constantly, 7 minutes or until sugar dissolves. Increase heat to high, and bring to a rolling boil, stirring often; boil, stirring constantly, 2 minutes. Turn off heat, and let stand, without stirring, 10 minutes. Skim off foam with a metal spoon.

3 Pour hot strawberry mixture into 5 (½-pt.) hot sterilized glass canning jars, filling to ¼ inch from top; wipe jar rims. Cover with lids, and screw on bands; cool completely (about 2 hours). Store in refrigerator up to 1 month.

Breakfast with Nannie + Papa

Trying apple butter for the first time remains one of my strongest culinary awakenings. I was sitting in Nannie and Papa's house, eating a drop biscuit. Most likely I wasn't going to finish my breakfast, so Daddy coated the remaining biscuit with a dark, mysterious substance—apple butter—and with my first bite, I was in love. Until that time, I had been finicky when it came to jams and preserves. Then I tasted the apple butter and everything changed. My parents, relieved to have finally found something I enjoyed, kept the fridge stocked from that moment forward.

Dutch Oven Apple Butter

I like to make my own apple butter, so that I know exactly what has gone into making this treat. I find that a mixture of sugars, along with some honey, provides the right amount of sweetness to counterbalance the tart apple flavors. For those who enjoy using a slow cooker, this recipe works just as well when the apples are cooked on HIGH for an hour or so then finished off for 10 or so hours on LOW. I just can't wait that long!

HANDS-ON 18 MIN. **TOTAL 4 HR., 48 MIN.**

MAKES 4 CUPS

1 Preheat oven to 350°. Heat an oven-safe Dutch oven over medium-high heat 1 minute or until hot. Add all ingredients, and stir until blended. Cook, stirring often, 15 minutes or until apples are tender.

2 Cover Dutch oven. Transfer to oven and bake, covered, at 350° for 4 hours, stirring every hour. Uncover and bake 15 more minutes or until mixture is reduced and thickened. Cool to room temperature (about 1½ hours). Store in refrigerator in tightly sealed sterilized glass canning jars or other airtight containers up to 1 month.

⋧ INGREDIENTS ⋦

2 Tbsp. unsalted butter
5⅓ lb. Granny Smith apples, peeled, cored, and thinly sliced (16 cups sliced)
1 cup light brown sugar
½ cup granulated sugar
½ cup clover honey
Pinch of salt
1 Tbsp. ground cinnamon

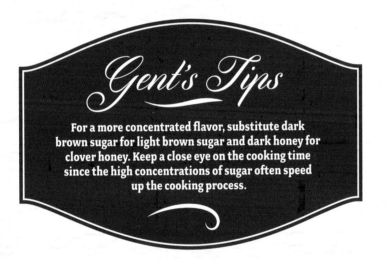

Gent's Tips

For a more concentrated flavor, substitute dark brown sugar for light brown sugar and dark honey for clover honey. Keep a close eye on the cooking time since the high concentrations of sugar often speed up the cooking process.

THE S.G.K. GUIDE

GLOSSARY

Whether you're an expert or a kitchen novice, a big part of nailing my recipes is understanding some of the following basic terms and cooking skills.

Al Dente — term used to describe cooked pasta, rice, or vegetables. Al dente is firm to the bite but not hard; a slight resistance occurs when chewed.

Bake — to cook by dry heat, especially in an oven.

Braise — to cook slowly in fat and moisture (stock, broth, wine, water).

Broil — to cook beneath direct high heat.

Chiffonade — to stack, roll, and finely slice greens or herbs into long thin strips.

Deglaze — to dissolve the small particles of sautéed solids remaining in a pan by adding liquid and heat. This is a crucial step when making soups, sauces, and pan reductions as the little browned bits left on the bottom of the pan after searing create rich flavors when dissolved into the liquid.

Direct Heat — to cook by direct exposure to the heat source.

To Dress — not a command for your wife or significant other. Instead, to season and/or add dressing to a salad, greens, or veggies.

Emulsify — to combine two or more liquids which will not combine, no matter how damn hard you try. Oil and vinegar, for example.

Fry — to cook in a pan or in a griddle over heat with the use of fat or oil.

Garnish — to add decorative or savory touches to enhance presentation or taste.

Grill — to cook by direct exposure on a heated grill rack above a fire or coals.

Indirect Heat — to cook by offsetting the heat source from the food. Most often used when smoking and slow cooking.

Julienne — to cut into long thin strips of the same size and thickness.

Kosher Salt — a natural form of salt that is larger in grain and more subtle in flavor than traditional salt. I like using large grain kosher salt due to its texture. Table salt can be substituted; 1 unit of table salt to 1½ units of kosher salt is generally a good rule for conversion.

On the Bias — to cut diagonally and across the grain, most typically when cutting meat.

To Plate — to arrange food on a plate, platter, or serving surface.

Poach — to cook in a simmering liquid.

Roux — flour and fat mixture used as a thickening agent, often referred to as 'Cajun Napalm' due to its danger in a kitchen. My recipes detail a low and slow technique for making a roux, which is the best way to ensure that you safely create this rich, nutty mixture without burning the batch, requiring you to start over. As you become more familiar with making roux, you can increase the heat to cut the cooking time roughly in half.

Sauté — to fry in a small amount of fat or oil.

To Taste — to add seasonings or ingredients suited to your preference, especially salt and pepper.

Whisk — to use a quick light brushing or whipping motion.

THE S.G.K. GUIDE

THE S.G.K. PANTRY

I enjoy visiting my farmers' markets to cook what is fresh, in-season, and oftentimes on sale. When I return home, it's nice to keep my kitchen stocked with the following basic raw materials so that I only have to pick up a few items with each stop at the market.

Oil and vinegar — keep in a cool, dry place; lasts from 6 months to 1 year.

Balsamic vinegar

White wine vinegar

Red wine vinegar

Extra virgin olive oil

Peanut oil

Dried spices and herbs — keep in a cool, dry place; 6 months.

Large grain kosher salt

Black pepper

Cajun Creole seasoning

Bay leaves

Crushed red pepper flakes

Condiments — follow product storage instructions.

Whole grain mustard

Ketchup

Mayonnaise

Local honey

Sorghum/molasses

Tabasco

CANNED GOODS — follow product storage instructions.

1 (16-oz.) can diced tomatoes

1 (15-oz.) can tomato sauce

1 (16-oz.) can tomato paste

DRY GOODS

All-purpose flour

Baking powder

Sugar

Converted rice

Stone ground grits

FRESH ITEMS

Large cage free eggs — 2 weeks refrigerated.

Unsalted Butter — 2-3 months refrigerated; freeze and thaw as needed up to 6 months.

Organic Whole Milk — follow product storage instructions.

Parmigiano-Reggiano Cheese — keeps up to a year when refrigerated and stored in a sealed bag. Freeze the rinds for adding flavor to soups, stocks, etc.

Lemons/limes

Heads of Garlic — 1 month refrigerated; 2-3 weeks in a cool, dry place.

Sweet onions — preferably Vidalia variety; 1 month in a cool, dry place.

Fresh Herbs (Basil, Parsley, Chives, Rosemary, Tarragon) — 5-6 days refrigerated; 3-4 days in a cool, dry place. Assuming you have the time and space, a potted plant of herbs or small herb garden is easy to maintain, not to mention a convenient and cheap way to ensure you have fresh herbs on hand.

THE S.G.K. GUIDE

S.G.K. GEAR

We Southern gentleman are known to adore our 'things.' Guns, tractors, collectibles, hunting and fishing gear, etc. It's part of our proper Southern upbringing to acquire only the finest of equipment for one's trade. Yet, in the kitchen, rather than be weighed down (and made broke) with a bunch and tools and gizmos, I prefer to keep things simple.

HARDWARE:
POTS/PANS/BAKING DISHES

12-inch Cast-Iron Skillet with Lid — cast-iron cookware is inexpensive, and it lasts a lifetime. On top of that, it cooks evenly, retains heat, and it is also believed to keep you healthy by supplying a steady dose of iron to your diet. Cast-iron cookware should never be placed in the dishwasher, nor should soap be used to clean the surface. Instead, rinse the cookware with hot water and, if necessary, use a nylon brush and kosher salt as an abrasive to remove any foods that stick to the surface. Coating the pan in a thin layer of oil in between use will help maintain the seasoned surface.

Cast-Iron Grill Pan — I realize not everyone has access to an outdoor grill, so this piece of equipment makes for an outstanding substitute. I prefer cast-iron grill pans over the non-stick versions. A grill pan can be used over high heat on the stovetop to create perfect grill marks, and it can be inserted into a heated oven to finish off thicker cuts that require more cooking time.

8-inch Oven-Safe Non-Stick Skillets with Glass Lid — non-stick cookware is a lifesaver when it comes to cooking items such as eggs. It's also a healthier way to cook, as less fat (butter/oils) is needed to prevent foods from sticking to the pan. Be sure to avoid using metal objects on the non-stick surface, otherwise they can cause damage to the cookware and reduce its effectiveness over time.

1 Large 6-qt. Oven-Safe Pot/Dutch Oven with Lid — perfect for making a large pot of grits or boiling potatoes.

1 Small 2.5-qt. Oven-Safe Pot with Lid — essential for making sauces, steaming vegetables, or heating liquids.

Large Pyrex or Enameled Cast-Iron Casserole Dish — a must have for baking or roasting.

Non-Stick Rimmed Baking Sheet — durable, cheap, and versatile. Always have a few of these readily available in your kitchen.

THE S.G.K. GUIDE

MORE TOOLS AND ACCESSORIES

8-inch Chef's Knife with a Sharpening Steel — splurge on a great knife, as this will be your most utilized tool in the kitchen.

Cutting Board — I prefer large wooden cutting boards over any other surface. If space allows, I like something that is at least 1.5 ft. x 1.5 ft. Several manufacturers also create a 'well' around the perimeter, which is nice to catch juices when slicing meat—keeping your countertops clean. Lastly, make sure it has a solid footing, so as not to slide while cutting.

Digital Instant-Read Thermometer — a useful tool to make sure cooking and internal temperatures are accurate.

Can Opener — always strive to use fresh ingredients, but when you cannot, this tool will come in handy.

Peppermill — indispensable for any kitchen. Though several manufacturers now offer 'disposable' peppermills, in the long run it's cheaper to buy a quality peppermill and fill it with whole peppercorns when needed.

Box Grater — I like this grater because it provides several different options in one; a slicer, a rough grate, a fine grate, and an extra fine grate for harder cheeses. Look for a grater with a large bottom base to provide more stability.

Vegetable Peeler — necessary for quickly peeling vegetables or shaving cheeses.

Immersion Blender/Food Processor — the workhorse of the kitchen. Great for saving time and creating specialized dishes.

Colander — a must have for draining, washing, straining, or rinsing.

Wooden Spoon — heatproof and durable, I like having these in several different sizes. These are also perfect when working with non-stick cookware.

Whisks — used to whisk together ingredients such as salad dressings, batters, etc.

Spatula — choose a slotted spatula, as they pick up the food while leaving any unnecessary grease behind.

Tongs — think of these as your mechanical arm. Stainless steel tongs provide precise control over your ingredients.

Pot Holder/Oven Mitt — necessary protection for handling hot cookware, such as cast iron. A folded towel will also do the trick.

Measuring Cups and Spoons — crucial for making the right measurements, especially when baking.

RESOURCES

Benton's Smoky Mountain Country Hams
Bacon, country hams, and did I say bacon!?
*bentonscountryhams2.com, 2603 Hwy. 411 N.
Madisonville, TN 37354, 423.442.5003*

Cajun Grocer
A one-stop shop for fresh crawfish, authentic
andouille, and other Cajun/Creole specialties;
cajungrocer.com, 888.CRAWFISH

Captain Jack Payne
The best 'character' of a fishing guide that puts
you right on the big reds!; Sweetwater Guide
Service & Marina; *delacroixfishing.com, 6205
Delacroix Hwy St. Bernard, LA 70085, 504.453.8382*

D'Artagnan
Online store for wild game including buffalo,
venison, boar, and an array of birds;
dartagnan.com, 800.327.8246

Ernest Pillow
My main man in Nashville for BBQ, smoked
turkey and hams served with a solid side of
humor; *615.578.1181*

Geechie Boy Market & Mill
Stone ground grits and cornmeal;
*geechieboymill.com, 2995 Hwy. 174 Edisto Island,
SC 29438, 843.209.5220*

Georgia Olive Farms
Locally grown and sourced high-quality olive
oil—liquid gold—from South Georgia;
georgiaolivefarms.com, 229.482.3505

Hashems
Online store for Middle East specialties such as
grape leaves, cheeses, breads, etc.; *hashems.com,
888.581.3212*

Kenny's Farmhouse Cheese
Artisan cheeses including American and
European varieties; *kennyscheese.com,
2033 Thomerson Park Rd. Austin, KY 42123,
888.571.4029*

Lazzaroli Pasta
Handmade pastas, sauces, and cheese by
my buddy Tom Lazzaro. Simply delicious;
*lazzaroli.com, 1314 5th Ave. N. #100 Nashville, TN
37208, 615.291.9922*

Lodge Cast Iron
Tennessee manufacturer of all things cast iron;
*lodgemfg.com, 503 South Cedar Ave. South
Pittsburgh, TN 37380, 423.837.7181*

Noble Springs Dairy
Locally sourced and curated goat cheese, milks,
and soaps from Dustin and Justyne Noble;
*noble-springs.com, 3144 Blazer Rd. Franklin, TN
37064, 615.481.9546*

Phickles
Small batch pickle company based in Athens,
GA. Seriously addicting!; *phickles.com, 100 Athens
Town Blvd. Athens, GA 30606, 706.338.6957*

Savannah Bee Company
Honey, skin care, and spirits—all the brainchild
of owner and gentleman Ted Dennard;
*savannahbee.com, 104 West Broughton St.
Savannah, GA 31401, 800.955.5080*

Saint Rita's Cakes
My Aunt Jeanne's bakery known for her
traditional southern pound cake and seasonal
varieties; *stritascakes.com, 404.435.3898*

Wild Georgia Shrimp
Georgia Shrimp Association marketing effort
to support shrimpers like Michael Sullivan;
wildgeorgiashrimp.com

METRIC EQUIVALENTS

The recipes that appear in this cookbook use the standard U.S. method for measuring liquid and dry or solid ingredients (teaspoons, tablespoons, and cups). The information on this chart is provided to help cooks outside the United States successfully use these recipes. All equivalents are approximate.

Metric Equivalents for Different Types of Ingredients

A standard cup measure of a dry or solid ingredient will vary in weight depending on the type of ingredient. A standard cup of liquid is the same volume for any type of liquid. Use the following chart when converting standard cup measures to grams (weight) or milliliters (volume).

Standard Cup	Fine Powder (ex. flour)	Grain (ex. rice)	Granular (ex. sugar)	Liquid Solids (ex. butter)	Liquid (ex. milk)
1	140 g	150 g	190 g	200 g	240 ml
³/₄	105 g	113 g	143 g	150 g	180 ml
²/₃	93 g	100 g	125 g	133 g	160 ml
¹/₂	70 g	75 g	95 g	100 g	120 ml
¹/₃	47 g	50 g	63 g	67 g	80 ml
¹/₄	35 g	38 g	48 g	50 g	60 ml
¹/₈	18 g	19 g	24 g	25 g	30 ml

Useful Equivalents for Liquid Ingredients by Volume

¹/₄ tsp					=	1 ml	
¹/₂ tsp					=	2 ml	
1 tsp					=	5 ml	
3 tsp	=	1 Tbsp		=	¹/₂ fl oz =	15 ml	
		2 Tbsp	=	¹/₈ cup =	1 fl oz =	30 ml	
		4 Tbsp	=	¹/₄ cup =	2 fl oz =	60 ml	
		5¹/₃ Tbsp	=	¹/₃ cup =	3 fl oz =	80 ml	
		8 Tbsp	=	¹/₂ cup =	4 fl oz =	120 ml	
		10²/₃ Tbsp	=	²/₃ cup =	5 fl oz =	160 ml	
		12 Tbsp	=	³/₄ cup =	6 fl oz =	180 ml	
		16 Tbsp	=	1 cup =	8 fl oz =	240 ml	
		1 pt	=	2 cups =	16 fl oz =	480 ml	
		1 qt	=	4 cups =	32 fl oz =	960 ml	
					33 fl oz =	1000 ml	= 1 l

Useful Equivalents for Dry Ingredients by Weight

(To convert ounces to grams, multiply the number of ounces by 30.)

1 oz	=	¹/₁₆ lb	=	30 g
4 oz	=	¹/₄ lb	=	120 g
8 oz	=	¹/₂ lb	=	240 g
12 oz	=	³/₄ lb	=	360 g
16 oz	=	1 lb	=	480 g

Useful Equivalents for Length

(To convert inches to centimeters, multiply the number of inches by 2.5.)

1 in				=	2.5 cm		
6 in	=	¹/₂ ft		=	15 cm		
12 in	=	1 ft		=	30 cm		
36 in	=	3 ft	=	1 yd =	90 cm		
40 in				=	100 cm	=	1 m

Useful Equivalents for Cooking/Oven Temperatures

	Fahrenheit	Celsius	Gas Mark
Freeze water	32° F	0° C	
Room temperature	68° F	20° C	
Boil water	212° F	100° C	
Bake	325° F	160° C	3
	350° F	180° C	4
	375° F	190° C	5
	400° F	200° C	6
	425° F	220° C	7
	450° F	230° C	8
Broil			Grill

INDEX

ACKNOWLEDGMENTS

First off, a huge thanks to my family, especially my mama, for helping me put this book together. I'm incredibly proud of our family history and heritage, not to mention our food! Thank you for allowing me the opportunity to share some of our beloved recipes with the rest of the world. The good Lord has his blessings!

To my loving wife, Callie. You are my girl. I appreciate your love and support throughout this creative endeavor. I love you (and the new Southern belle we'll soon welcome into the world!).

To my friends near and far, thank you for sheltering me during my travels, as well as always bringing your hearty appetites when it's time to taste my recipes! Many more great meals await y'all.

My agent, Stacey Glick—for your belief in my writing and constant support throughout the years. I could not have done this without you—cheers to many more!

My editor, Erica Sanders-Foege, thank you for giving me the confidence to speak in my own voice. You've been a champion of this book since the beginning—I truly thank you. To Allison Cox Vasquez, the photography team, and to the test kitchen all-stars—y'all have carefully refined and curated all of my recipes to ensure this will be a book that folks will actually cook from—accomplishing my most important goal!

Hunter Holder, your incredible lifestyle photography, friendship, and willingness to always grab a cold beer is truly appreciated. To Sid Evans, Margot Schupf, Susan Hettleman, Courtney Greenhalgh, Felicity Keane, Hunter Lewis, Jim Childs, Leah McLaughlin, and Lindsay Bierman and the rest of the team at Time Home Entertainment and *Southern Living*—many talented folks and resources went into bringing this book to life. Y'all have outdone yourselves!

I'd also like to thank some specific folks who went above and beyond to make this book possible: Greg Arnette, Kris Koller, Brett McKay, Kyah Hillis, Matt Barnett, Jeff Francoeur, Luke Bryan, Dave Haywood, Jon Stinchcomb, Ted Dennard, Ernest Pillow, Thad Cockrell, C.B. Ozburn, Kerri Edwards, Lamar Moore, Emily Breland, Daniel Perkins, Mark Turner, Jason Shaw, Michael Sullivan, Tom Lazzaro, Captain Jack, and all the rest who played their role—y'all keep peaceful!

ISBN-13: 978-0-8487-4367-3
ISBN-10: 0-8487-4367-9
Library of Congress Control Number:
2014959112

Printed in the United States of America
First Printing 2015

Oxmoor House

Creative Director: Felicity Keane
Art Director: Christopher Rhoads
Executive Photography Director: Iain Bagwell
Executive Food Director: Grace Parisi
Senior Editor: Erica Sanders-Foege
Managing Editor: Elizabeth Tyler Austin
Assistant Managing Editor:
 Jeanne de Lathouder

PHOTO CREDITS:

Matt Barnett: 89, 260; Hunter Holder: 2, 8, 13, 83, 125, 220; Skip Hopkins: 11; Vicki Shaw: 67; Becky Luigart-Stayner: 286; Other lifestyle photography provided by Matt Moore

Cover Design:
Steve Attardo/NINETYNORTH Design

A Southern Gentleman's Kitchen

Associate Editor: Allison Cox Vasquez
Assistant Project Editor: Lacie Pinyan
Editorial Assistant: April Smitherman
Assistant Designer: Allison Sperando Potter
Assistant Test Kitchen Manager:
 Alyson Moreland Haynes
Recipe Developers and Testers:
 Stefanie Maloney; Callie Nash; Karen Rankin
Food Stylists: Nathan Carrabba,
 Victoria E. Cox, Margaret Monroe Dickey,
 Catherine Crowell Steele
Photo Editor: Kellie Lindsey
Senior Photographer: Hélène Dujardin
Senior Photo Stylists: Kay E. Clarke,
 Mindi Shapiro Levine
Senior Production Managers: Greg A. Amason,
 Sue Chodakiewicz

Contributors

Writer: Matt Moore
Designer: Steve Attardo/NINETYNORTH Design
Executive Editor: Katherine Cobbs
Illustrator: Steven Noble
Copy Editors: Norma McKittrick, Cathy Fowler
Proofreader: Adrienne Davis, Barry Wise Smith
Indexer: Mary Ann Laurens
Fellows: Laura Arnold, Kylie Dazzo,
 Nicole Fisher, Loren Lorenzo, Anna Ramia,
 Caroline Smith, Amanda Widis
Photographers: Matt Barnett, Hunter Holder,
 Skip Hopkins, Vicki Shaw, Becky Luigart-Stayner
Photo Stylists: Cindy Barr, Lydia DeGaris Pursell

Time Home Entertainment Inc.

Publisher: Margot Schupf
Vice President, Finance: Vandana Patel
Executive Director, Marketing Services:
 Carol Pittard
Publishing Director: Megan Pearlman
Assistant General Counsel: Simone Procas